THE WELCOMING CHURCH: CHRISTIAN INITIATION

A HANDBOOK OF LITURGICAL AND PATRISTIC SOURCES

THE WELCOMING CHURCH: CHRISTIAN INITIATION

A HANDBOOK OF LITURGICAL AND PATRISTIC SOURCES

Compiled with Introductions

by

JOHN J. BEGLEY, S.J.

SCRANTON: UNIVERSITY OF SCRANTON PRESS

Produced with the
support of the University of
Scranton Jesuit Community

Library of Congress Cataloging-in-Publication Data

Christian initiation : a handbook of sources / compiled with introductions
by John J. Begley.
    p.cm.
Includes bibliographical references and index.
ISBN 0-940866-90-0 (pbk.)
    1. Initiation rites--Religious aspects--Catholic Church--History of
doctrines--Sources.
  I. Begley, John J., 1931 -

  BX2045.155 C48 2000
  264'.0208'09--dc21

                                                              00-034361

Distribution:
University of Scranton Press
Chicago Distribution Center
11030 S. Langley
Chicago IL 60628

TABLE OF CONTENTS

INTRODUCTION

The purpose of this modest collection of liturgical and patristic sources for the sacraments of baptism, confirmation, and Eucharist is to provide easy access to beginning students to the sources which document the richness of their sacramental heritage. There are, to be sure, other such collections concerned with one or another of these sacraments, such as that by Whitaker for baptism (*Documents of the Baptismal Liturgy*), Jasper and Cuming for the Eucharist (*Prayers of the Eucharist: Early and Reformed*), and Yarnold for the witness of the Fathers of the Church of the fourth century (*The Awe Inspiring Rites of Initiation*). However, no one collection is available which brings the scriptural, liturgical, and patristic sources together in a form accessible to students. It is that need, experienced in the university classroom, which this present collection attempts to meet.

The original intent was to provide a text complete with the kind of useful notes and critical analysis that characterize the works mentioned above. Subsequent classroom instruction and discussion with students made it clear that however important such a resource would be for the scholar or advanced student, those who are beginning the study of sacraments are intimidated and discouraged by such scholarship.

With the exception of pertinent parts of the account of her pilgrimage by the remarkable woman, Egeria, excerpts from the informative letter of the Deacon John, and of course, the New Testament and the contemporary *Rite of Christian Initiation of Adults*, all texts are either actual liturgical texts or homilies by a major figure of the Church and date from before or very close to the end of the fourth century when the rites had achieved maturity and before their subsequent and unfortunate dissolution.

Each of the texts is preceded by an introduction which attempts to provide at least a probable date for its origin, to identify, where possible, its author, and to indicate some aspects of the text which illustrate its importance.

The bibliography for the topic of initiation is seemingly endless. Here the brief appended bibliography includes only those sources and secondary literature which were used repeatedly in the preparation of the collection and the introductions and which are readily available to students.

I wish to thank Richard W. Rousseau, S.J., who guided an earlier version of this collection to completion, Edward Yarnold, S.J., who read the first version with great care and made a number of saving suggestions, and Robert Kelly, editor of Geoffrey Chapman, for his continuing interest and editorial skill. The present collection is much improved because of their help and interest.

Finally, I wish to thank Patty Mecadon of the University of Scranton Press for all her help in preparing the manuscript for publication, and the Jesuit Community of the University whose subsidy made publication possible.

Pentecost 2000   John J. Begley, S.J.

ACKNOWLEDGMENTS

Grateful acknowledgment is extended to the following publishers for permission to use these translations either in whole or in part; Catholic University of America Press for translations from *The Didache*, *The First Apology* of Justin, the *De Sacramentis* of Saint Ambrose, *The Mystagogical Lectures* of Saint Cyril of Jerusalem, which appear in the series, *The Fathers of the Church*, in Vol. 1, pp. 177, 178–180, 182–183; Vol. 6, pp. 99–100, 104–107; Vol. 44, pp. 269–295; Vol. 64, pp. 153–203; Alba House for translations of the *Anaphoras of Saint Basil and of Saint John Chrysostom* in *The Mass: Ancient Liturgies and Patristic Texts*, pp. 70–77; and the Roman Canon in Cipriano Vagaggini, *The Canon of the Mass and Liturgical Reform*, pp. 331–334; The Liturgical Press for translations of *The Apostolic Tradition* of Hippolytus, the *Anaphora of Addai and Mari*, *The Euchologion* of Serapion, *The Apostolic Constitutions*, in *Early Sources of the Liturgy*, pp. 37–41, 43–47, 52–64, 113–118, 122–129, 152, 157–158, 161–164, 169–174, 178–183, (reprinted as *Springtime of the Liturgy* with a different chapter ordering); and the *Baptismal Homilies* of Theodore of Mopsuestia in Edward Yarnold, *The Awe-Inspiring Rites of Initiation*, pp. 168–243, 250. The Paulist Press for *The Second Instruction* of John Chrysostom in *St. John Chrysostom: Baptismal Instructions*, pp. 43–55 of Vol. 31, and *Diary of a Pilgrimage*, pp. 113–114, 122–126 of Vol. 38 in the series *Ancient Christian Writers*; S.P.C.K. for the translation of *Letter to Senarius* in E. C. Whitaker, *Documents of the Baptismal Liturgy*, pp. 144–148; the International Committee on English in the Liturgy for excerpts from the English translation of *Rite of Christian Initiation of Adults* © 1988, International Committee on the Liturgy, Inc. All Rights Reserved. The Scripture quotations contained herein are from the New Revised Standard Version Bible, copyright © 1989 by the Division of Christian Education of The National Council of Churches in the U.S.A., and are used by permission. All rights reserved.

CHAPTER ONE

THE SACRAMENTS OF INITIATION IN
THE NEW TESTAMENT

BAPTISM

Baptism is mentioned rarely in the Gospels, and the distinction between baptism and confirmation does not occur until centuries after the New Testament. Baptism is used as a metaphor for the passion and death of Jesus (Lk 12:50). The need of baptism is stressed in the conversation between Jesus and Nicodemus (Jn 3:5), and the importance of baptism in the ministry of the Church is traced back to a command of the Risen Lord (Mt 28:19; Mk 16:16), although in the judgment of most scholars the command is clearly influenced by the liturgy, and the formula in the "long ending" of Mark is from the second century.

Ritual washing was common in Judaism and other religions of the time. While most of the washing looked to the removal of ritual impurity, there are clear associations of God cleansing with water and bringing about interior personal renewal and the giving of God's own spirit (Ez 36:21–27; Ps 51). Proselyte baptism within Judaism would have provided a rich store of images and understanding for early Christian catechesis. The activity of the Baptist, for all its uniqueness, was part of a widespread movement. The apostles baptized, although it is unclear whether Jesus himself baptized (Jn 3:22; 4:2). For many, 1 Pet 1:3–2:10 is a baptismal homily in which the new Christians' former state is contrasted with their present state brought about by baptism.

Jesus' baptism by John is the prototype of Christian baptism, although it must be noted that both the experience of Pentecost and contemporary liturgical practice probably influenced the account of Jesus' baptism. As Jesus was anointed by the Holy Spirit, so all who follow him will receive the same Spirit, and as Jesus is declared God's "Beloved Son," so his followers will also be declared sons and

1

daughters. There is no conclusive evidence in the New Testament of a particular ritual act, either the laying on of hands or of an anointing, which symbolized the gift of the Spirit. The evidence for laying on of hands is stronger than that for anointing.

The sequence of events in the New Testament is invariable. The gospel is proclaimed, conversion takes place and leads to baptism, and the neophyte enters into the life and activity of the Spirit-filled community. The very rich meaning of baptism is indicated in the texts provided here which present a variety of interpretations of the one rite: it brings about the forgiveness of sins and bestows the Holy Spirit (1 Cor 6:11, 19), it is a sign of the unity of believers (Eph 4:5), all of whom were called to live the very life of Christ (Gal 3:27); it plunged the catechumen into Christ's death and became the demand for a new life, following the pattern of the Risen Lord (Rom 6:3–5), was a new birth (Jn 3:5), a seal (2 Cor 1:22; Eph 1:13; 4:30) an illumination (Eph 5:8–14), a new circumcision (Col 2:11), a bath of regeneration (Ti 3:5), and to be in Christ was to be a new creation (2 Cor 5:17). Although Paul's mature understanding of baptism as incorporation into the paschal mystery of the death-resurrection of Christ is not prominent in the earliest liturgical documents, it is the understanding of baptism which has dominated Christian thinking about baptism in the West throughout subsequent centuries. In the East, however, in early Syria and Egypt, it is the baptism of Jesus in the Jordan, in which is manifested the gift of the Holy Spirit and adoption as God's beloved children, which is the central paradigm.

TEXTS

1 Corinthians 6:11

And such were some of you. But you were washed, you were sanctified, you were justified in the name of the Lord Jesus Christ and in the Spirit of our God.

1 Corinthians 6:19

Do you not know that your body is a temple of the Holy Spirit within you, which you have from God? You are not your own.

Galatians 3:25–4:7

But now that faith has come, we are no longer under a custodian, 26. for in Christ Jesus you are all sons of God, through faith. 27. For as many of you as were baptized into Christ have put on Christ. 28. There is neither Jew nor Greek, there is neither slave nor free, there is neither male nor female; for you are all one in Christ Jesus. 29. And if you are Christ's, then you are Abraham's offspring, heirs according to promise. 4:1. I mean that the heir, as long as he is a child, is no better than a slave, though he is the owner of all the estate; 2. but he is under guardians and trustees until the date set by the father. 3. So with us; when we were children, we were slaves to the elemental spirits of the universe. 4. But when the time had fully come, God sent forth his Son, born of woman, born under the law, 5. to redeem those who were under the law, so that we might receive adoption as sons. 6. And because you are sons, God has sent the Spirit of his Son into our hearts, crying, "Abba! Father!" 7. So through God you are no longer a slave but a son, and if a son then an heir.

Romans 6:1–11

What shall we say then? Are we to continue in sin that grace may abound? 2. By no means! How can we who died to sin still live in it? 3. Do you not know that all of us who have been baptized into Christ Jesus were baptized into his death? 4. We were buried therefore with him by baptism into death, so that a Christ was raised from the dead by the glory of the Father, we too might walk in newness of life. 5. For if we have been united with him in a death like his, we shall certainly be united with him in a resurrection like his. 6. We know that our old self was crucified with him so that the sinful body might be destroyed, and we might no longer be enslaved to sin. 7. For he who has died is freed from sin. 8. But if we have died with Christ, we believe that we shall also live with him. 9. For we know that Christ being raised from the dead will never die again; death no longer has dominion over him. 10. The death he died he died to sin, once for all, but the life he lives he lives to God. 11. So you also must consider yourselves dead to sin and alive to God in Christ Jesus.

Colossians 2:11–13

In him also you were circumcised with a circumcision made without hands, by putting off the body of flesh in the circumcision of

Christ; 12. and you were buried with him in baptism, in which you were also raised with him through faith in the working of God, who raised him from the dead. 13. And you, who were dead in trespasses and the uncircumcision of your flesh, God made alive together with him, having forgiven us all our trespasses.

Gal 3:27

For as many of you as were baptized into Christ have put on Christ.

Ephesians 1:13

In him you also, who have heard the word of truth, the gospel of your salvation, and have believed in him, were sealed with the promised Holy Spirit.

Ephesians 4:5

There is one Lord, one faith, one baptism.

Ephesians 4:30

And do not grieve the Holy Spirit of God, in whom you were sealed for the day of redemption.

Ephesians 5:8–9

For once you were darkness, but now you are light in the Lord; walk as children of light 9. (for the fruit of light is found in all that is good and right and true).

Ephesians 2:4–6

But God, who is rich in mercy, out of the great love with which he loved us, 5. even when we were dead through our trespasses, made us alive together with Christ (by grace you have been saved), 6. and raised us up with him, and made us sit with him in the heavenly places in Christ Jesus.

1 Peter 3:21

Baptism . . . now saves you, not as a removal of dirt from the body but as an appeal to God for a clear conscience, through the resurrection of Jesus Christ.

Titus 3:5

He saved us, not because of deeds done by us in righteousness, but in virtue of his own mercy, by the washing of regeneration and renewal in the Holy Spirit.

THE EUCHARIST

The origin of the Christian celebration of the Eucharist, Jesus' Last Supper with his disciples, is related by the Synoptics (Mt 26:26–29; Mk 14:22–25; Lk 22:14–20) and also by Paul (1 Cor. 11:23–26). The gospel of John does not mention the Eucharist in his account of the Last Supper but does provide a profound theology of "The Eucharist" in the context of a feeding miracle (Jn 6:51–58). The similarities in the accounts are obvious but there are also some less obvious differences in them. First, the command to "Do this in memory of me" appears in Luke and twice in Paul but not in Mark or Matthew. Mark-Matthew identify the contents of the cup; Luke-Paul refer to the cup itself. All four have the same sequence of verbs; took the bread, gave thanks or pronounced the blessing, broke the bread, gave the bread and the cup to his disciples. The verb gave does not appear but is implied in Paul's account. There is an obvious connection between the actions of Jesus at the Last Supper and the miraculous feeding of the five thousand recorded in all of the Gospels (Mk 6:41–44; Mt 14:15–21; Lk 9:12–17; Jn 6:1–15). The miraculous feeding itself recalls God's feeding of His people in the wilderness and Elisha's feeding of one hundred men (2 Kings 4:42–44). The similarity of phrases in the two Gospel accounts indicates the early community's Eucharistic understanding of the feeding of the multitudes. The sequence of verbs is also reflected in the structure of the contemporary liturgy of the Eucharist in which first, the gifts are prepared; second, the Eucharistic prayer is offered within which occurs the narrative of institution; third, the breaking of bread; and fourth, communion. There are, as could be expected in a matter of such importance, questions about the accounts of the Last Supper which remain unanswered despite the advances of scholarship. For example, is the chronology of the Synoptics according to which Jesus celebrates his Last Supper on Passover, to be preferred to that of John, according to which Jesus celebrates his Last Supper the day before Passover? The question will probably never be answered, although at the present time it is recognized that theological concerns are behind the time frames provided both by John and the Synoptics. However the question of chronology is answered, it remains an open question whether Jesus celebrated Passover with his disciples or whether the evangelists have supplied the Passover setting. Further, are the words of institution, "This is my body. This is my blood," the words of Jesus himself? Or is the origin of the words of institution to be sought in the earliest Christian communities? However this question may be answered, the origins of the Eucharist are to be located in Jesus himself. It is impossible to explain how the earliest communities could simply have invented the Eucharistic practice so soon after the death of Jesus.

There are two traditions of the institution at the Last Supper: that of Mark who is followed very closely by Matthew, and that of Paul, which appears to have influenced the account in Luke. Mark-Matthew stresses the inauguration of the New Covenant in the atoning blood of Jesus. Paul-Luke stresses the Eucharist as the Passover of the New Covenant. Mark-Matthew must be read against the background of the following texts concerning the covenant in the Jewish Scriptures: Ex 24:4–8; Zech 9:9–11; Jer 31:31–34; Is 52:13–53; 12. Paul-Luke must be read against the background of the institution of Passover in Ex 12:1–14, 21–28. The structure of the accounts with their repetition of the same four key verbs indicates that the writers were repeating a memorized text which was familiar to them from their own participation in the Eucharist. Two of the verbs have been used to refer to the entire rite, "Eucharist" (blessed) and "the breaking of bread" (broke). While Luke-Paul is the older written account, it does not necessarily represent an earlier account than Mark-Matthew. Luke's account bears comparison to Jewish festive meals and may represent a time when the Eucharist was celebrated within the context of a meal, and the latter with its symmetry between the words over the bread and the cup may represent a time when the Eucharist, for the reasons which occasioned Paul's account, had already been separated from a meal. John's gospel account of the Last Supper contains no mention of the institution of the Eucharist. John's theology of the Eucharist is contained in c.6. The Last Supper account in this gospel, as also in Luke, presents Jesus' farewell address, his last will and testament. Of particular importance here is the example given by Jesus in washing the feet of his disciples, and the command, "So, if I, your Lord and Teacher, have washed your feet, you also ought to wash one another's feet. For I have set you an example, that you also should do as I have done to you" (13:14–15). A necessary condition for participating in the memorial of the Lord's death and resurrection is the loving service of others.

TEXTS

INSTITUTION NARRATIVES

Mark 14:22–25

And as they were eating, he took bread, and blessed, and broke it, and gave it to them, and said, "Take: this is my body." 23. And he took a cup, and when he had given thanks he gave it to them, and they all drank of it. 24. And he said to them, "This is my blood of the covenant, which is poured out for many. Truly, I say to you, I shall not drink again of the fruit of the vine until that day when I drink it new in the kingdom of God."

Luke 22:14, 15, 19–20

And when the hour came, he sat at table, and the apostles with him. 15. And he said to them, "I have earnestly desired to eat this Passover with you before I suffer. 16. For I tell you I shall not eat it until it is fulfilled in the kingdom of God. 19. And he took bread, and when he had given thanks he broke it and gave it to them, saying, "This is my body which is given for you. Do this in remembrance of me." 20. And likewise the cup after supper, saying, "This cup which is poured out for you is the new covenant in my blood."

Matthew 26:26–28

Now as they were eating, Jesus took bread, and blessed, and broke it, and gave it to the disciples and said, "Take, eat; this is my body." 27. And he took a cup, and when he had given thanks he gave it to them saying, "Drink of it, all of you; 28. For this is my blood of the covenant, which is poured out for many for the forgiveness of sins. 29. I tell you I shall not drink of this fruit of the vine until that day when I drink it new with you in my Father's kingdom."

1 Corinthians 11: 23–26

For I received from the Lord what I also delivered to you, that the Lord Jesus on the night when he was betrayed took bread, 24. And when he had given thanks, he broke it, and said, "This is my body which is for you. Do this in remembrance of me." 25. In the same way also the cup, after supper, saying, "This cup is the new covenant in my blood. Do this, as often as you drink it, in remembrance of me. 26. For as often as you eat this bread and drink the cup, you proclaim the Lord's death until he comes."

John 6:51–58

I am the living bread which came down from heaven; if anyone eats of this bread, he will live for ever; and the bread which I shall give for the life of the world is my flesh. 52. The Jews then disputed among themselves, saying, "How can this man give us his flesh to eat?" 53. So Jesus said to them, "Truly, truly, I say to you, unless you eat the flesh of the Son of man and drink his blood, you have no life in you; 54. He who eats my flesh and drinks my blood has eternal life, and I will raise him up at the last day. 55. For my flesh is food indeed, and my blood is drink indeed. 56. He who eats my flesh and drinks my blood abides in me, and I in him. 57. As the living Father sent me, and I live because of the Father, so he who eats me will live because of me. 58. This is the bread which came down from heaven, not such as the fathers ate and died; he who eats this bread will live for ever."

John 13:1–15, 34

Now before the feast of the Passover when Jesus knew that his hour had come to depart out of this world to the Father, having loved his own who were in the world, he loved them to the end. 2. And during supper, when the devil had already put it into the heart of Judas Iscariot, Simon's son, to betray him, 3. Jesus, knowing that the Father had given all things into his hands, and that he had come from God and was going to God, 4. Rose from supper, laid aside his garments, and girded himself with a towel. 5. Then he poured water into a basin, and began to wash the disciples' feet, and to wipe them with the towel with which he was girded. 6. He came to Simon Peter; and Peter said to him, "Lord, do you wash my feet?" 7. Jesus answers him, "What I am doing you do not know now, but afterward you will understand." 8. Peter said to him, "You shall never wash my feet."

Jesus answered him, "If I do not wash you, you have no part in me."
9. Simon Peter said to him, "Lord, not my feet only but also my hands
and my head!" 10. Jesus said to him, "He who has bathed does not
need to wash, except his feet, but he is clean all over; and you are
clean, but not every one of you." 11. For he knew who was to betray
him; that was why he said, "You are not all clean." 12. When he had
washed their feet, and taken his garments, and resumed his place, he
said to them, "Do you know what I have done to you? 13. You call
me Teacher and Lord; and you are right, for so I am. 14. If I then,
Your Lord and Teacher, have washed your feet, you also ought to
wash one another's feet. 15. For I have given you an example, that
you also should do as I have done to you. 34. A new commandment
I give to you, that you love one another; even as I have loved you,
that you also love one another."

CHAPTER TWO

THE DIDACHE

*There is a consensus among historians of the liturgy that **The Didache** is the oldest liturgical document that we possess and is of singular importance for the study of the liturgy. However, this same consensus does not extend to the time or place in which it was written or even the precise nature of the specifically liturgical passages within it. This lack of agreement is due to the composite nature of the document which underwent revisions and probably additions during the course of its transmission. It was considered as scripture by some of the early Fathers but was lost to the modern world until 1883 when it was rediscovered and published from a manuscript dated 1056. Scholars point to various locations as the place of origin: Syria, Palestine, and Egypt are possible places. The date of its origin is placed as early as the middle of the first century, contemporaneous with the writing of St. Paul and the "Sayings Collection" (commonly referred to as "Q") which precedes the Gospels, or as late as the end of the second or the beginning of the third century. For some, the church order presupposed in **The Didache** makes it difficult to find any plausible place for it other than the period C.E. 70–110. It has been noted that **The Didache** may be oddly placed in this time period, but it would be even odder placed anywhere else. It seems probable that **The Didache**'s early chapters, because of their pro-nouncedly Jewish character, originated in a diaspora context such as Antioch in Syria.*

*The sections reproduced here, cc. 7, 9–10, 14, are those which treat of Baptism and the Eucharist. The following characteristics of the document are worth noting. It is the only document from the early centuries of the Church which mentions baptism by infusion. All other documents speak only of baptism by immersion. The theology of the Holy Spirit, mentioned only in the formula accompanying the rite, is relatively undeveloped. No mention is made of any gesture, either anointing or laying on of hands as symbolic of the gift of the Holy Spirit to the baptized. Also, as will be noted as well in Justin's **Apology*** *and The Apostolic Tradition of Hippolytus, the wording of the Eucharistic Prayer is left to the spontaneous devotion of the presider. In the prayers accompanying the Eucharist there is no reference to the redemptive death and resurrection of Jesus. Is it possible that the sequence of cup-bread, rather than the usual sequence bread-cup, reflects early practice (see Cor 10:16–17). Scholarly opinion is divided over the precise nature of cc. 9–10. Are these beautiful prayers which accompanied the Eucharist or were they said in the context of an Agape, a meal which the primitive Church originally celebrated in conjunction with the Eucharist but which was separated from it at an early date? However this question may eventually be answered, it is indisputable that these prayers are among the most beautiful of the Church's inheritance.*

[Translation, *FC*, I, pp. 177, 178–180, 182–183]

THE DIDACHE: TEXTS

BAPTISM

c. 7. Regarding baptism, baptize thus:

After giving the foregoing instructions, "Baptize in the name of the Father, and of the Son, and of the Holy Spirit" in running water. But, if you have no running water, baptize in any other; and, if you cannot in cold water, then in warm. But if the one is lacking, pour the other three times on the head. "In the name of the Father, and Son, and Holy Spirit." But before baptizing, let the one who baptizes and the one to be baptized fast, and any others who are able to do so. And you shall require the person being baptized to fast for one or two days.

THE EUCHARISTIC PRAYER

c. 9. In regard to the Eucharist, you shall offer the Eucharist thus:

First, in connection with the cup,
We give Thee thanks, our Father,
for the holy vine of David your Son,
which thou has made known to us through Jesus, your Son;
Glory to you forever.

And in connection with the breaking of bread,
We give you thanks, Our Father,
for the life and knowledge
you have revealed to us through Jesus, your Son;
Glory to you forever.

As this broken bread
was scattered over the mountain tops
and after being harvested was made one,
so let your Church be gathered together
from the ends of the earth into your kingdom,
for through Jesus Christ glory and power are yours forever.

But let no one eat or drink of the Eucharist
with you except those baptized in the name of the Lord,
for in reference to this the Lord said:
"Do not give that which is holy to dogs."

c. 10. After it has been completed, give thanks in the following way:
We thank you, Holy Father,
for thy Holy Name,
which you have caused to dwell in our hearts,
and for the knowledge, faith and immortality,
which you have made known to us through Jesus, Your Son.
Glory to You forever.

You, Lord Almighty, have created all
for Your name's sake,
and have given food and drink
that gives eternal life,
through Jesus, Your Son.

For all things we give you thanks,
because you are mighty;
Glory to You forever.

Remember, Lord, your Church,
deliver it from evil,
make it perfect in your love,
gather it from the four winds,
sanctified for your kingdom,

which you have prepared for it,
for Yours is the power and glory forever.

Let grace come, and let this world pass away,
Hosanna to the God of David.
If any one is holy, let him come;
If anyone is not, let him repent.
Marana tha! Amen.

(Allow the "prophets" to hold the Eucharist as they desire.)

THE SUNDAY EUCHARIST

c. 14. And on the Lord's Day, after you have come together, break bread and offer the Eucharist, having first confessed your offenses, so that your sacrifice may be pure. But let no one who has a quarrel with his neighbor join you until he is reconciled, lest your sacrifice be defiled. For it was said by the Lord; "In every place and time let there be offered to me a clean sacrifice, because I am the great king"; and also; "and my name is wonderful among the Gentiles" (Mal 1.11; 14).

CHAPTER THREE

THE APOLOGY OF JUSTIN MARTYR

*Justin is a central figure in the history of Christian thought of the second century. Referred to as the "Christian Philosopher" because of an openness to philosophy, which was not generally shared by his Christian contemporaries, he was born in the early years of the second century of Greek parents in the Samaritan territory. In his early years he was a student of philosophy but was dissuaded from further philosophical studies because one of his teachers insisted on receiving his fee for instruction. He is remarkable for his generous, open approach to the Greek philosophical tradition, his liberal and irenic spirit, and for the influence he exercised over Athenagoras of Athens, Clement of Alexandria, Theophilus and Irenaeus. His **Apology**, directed to the Emperor Antoninus Pius (138–161), is an explanation and defense of the outlawed Christian faith. Justin hoped to persuade the Emperor that Christians posed no threat to the Roman Empire but rather were good citizens. Eventually apprehended and tried for his adherence to Christianity, he was martyred between 162 and 168. His **Apology** was written some ten to fifteen years earlier in C.E. 151.*

*It is fortunate for us that in the interest of persuading the Emperor of the compatibility of being both devoted Christian and Roman citizen, Justin did not observe the **disciplina arcani**, the practice of not revealing any details about the liturgical rituals of Christian communities. His account provides us with some description of how the celebration of the sacraments of initiation were actually carried out in the middle of the second century. Interestingly, Justin uses the common term "illumination" for baptism, but, in terms perhaps owing to his philosophical training, he interprets "illumination" to mean intellectual understanding rather than salvation as was common. As his description of baptism refers to the "same manner in which we ourselves were regenerated" (c.61), it is clear that the manner of baptizing had already received some ritual consistency. Since he cites John's gospel*

(3:3), it is obvious that he was familiar with it. It appears that immediately after baptism, the neophytes were brought to the place where the Eucharist was to be celebrated. The Emperor is informed that in this early form of the "Prayer of the Faithful" the Christians prayed that they would be considered "as good citizens and observers of the [Roman] law" (c.65). Christians celebrate the Eucharist doing "what Jesus ordered them to do" (c.66). The much later theological explanation of "transubstantiation" is foreshadowed in Justin's remarkable analogy of the Incarnation of the Word and the Eucharist. In his description of the more ordinary Sunday celebration (c.67), the basic structure of the Eucharist, consisting of a "Liturgy of the Word," and "Liturgy of the Eucharist," as we know it today, is evident. Finally, it may be noted that twice Justin remarks about the importance of practical fraternal love within the community.

[Translation: *FC*, VI, pp. 99–100, 104–107]

THE FIRST APOLOGY

CHRISTIAN INITIATION

c.61 Lest we be judged unfair in this exposition, we will not fail to explain how we consecrated ourselves to God when we were regenerated through Christ.

Those who are convinced and believe what we say and teach is the truth, and pledge themselves to be able to live accordingly, are taught in prayer and fasting to ask God to forgive their past sins, while we pray and fast with them.

Then we lead them to a place where there is water, and they are regenerated in the same manner in which we ourselves were regenerated. In the name of God, the Father and Lord of all, and of our Savior, Jesus Christ, and of the Holy Spirit, they then receive the washing with water. For Christ said: "Unless you be born again, you shall not enter into the kingdom of heaven." Now it is clear to everyone how impossible it is for those who have been born once to enter their mothers' wombs again. Isaiah the Prophet explained, as we already stated, how those who have sinned and then repented shall be freed of their sins. These are his words: "Wash yourselves, be clean, banish sin from your souls; learn to do good. Judge for the fatherless and defend the widow; and then come and let us reason together, says the Lord. And if your sins be as scarlet, I will make them white as wool; and if they be red as crimson, I will make them white as snow. But if you do not hear Me, the sword shall devour you: for the mouth of the Lord has spoken it" (Is 1. 18–20). And this is the reason, taught to us by the Apostles, why we baptize the way we do. . . .

There is invoked over the one who wishes to be regenerated, and who is repentant of his sins, the name of God, the Father and Lord of all. . . .

This washing is called illumination, since they who learn these things become illuminated intellectually.

Furthermore, the illuminated one is also baptized in the name of Jesus Christ, who was crucified under Pontius Pilate, and in the name of the Holy Spirit, who predicted through the Prophets everything concerning Jesus.

THE CELEBRATION OF THE EUCHARIST

[The Community Prayers]

c.65 After thus baptizing the one who has believed and given his assent, we escort him to the place where are assembled those whom we call brethren, to offer up sincere prayers in common for ourselves, for the baptized person, and for all other persons wherever they may be, in order that, since we have found the truth we may be deemed fit through our actions to be esteemed as good citizens and observers of the law, and thus attain eternal salvation.

[The Kiss of Peace]

At the conclusion of the prayers we greet one another with a kiss [of peace].

[Anaphora]

Then, bread and a chalice containing wine mixed with water are presented to the one presiding over the brethren.

He takes them and offers praise and glory to the Father of them all, through the name of the Son and of the Holy Spirit, and he recites lengthy prayers of thanksgiving to God in the name of those to whom He granted such favors.

At the end of these prayers and thanksgiving, all present express their approval by saying, "Amen." This Hebrew word, "Amen," means "So be it."

[Communion]

When he who presides has celebrated the Eucharist, and all the people have expressed their approval, they whom we call deacons permit each one present to partake of the Eucharistic bread, and wine and water; and they carry it also to the absentees.

c.66 We call this food the Eucharist, of which only he can partake who has acknowledged the truth of our teachings, who has been cleansed by baptism for the remission of his sins and for his regeneration, and who regulates his life upon the principles laid down by Christ. Not as ordinary bread or as ordinary drink do we partake of them, but just as, through the word of God, our Savior Jesus Christ became Incarnate and took upon Himself flesh and blood for our salvation, so we have been taught, the food which has been made the Eucharist by the prayer of His word, and which nourishes our flesh and blood by assimilation, is both the flesh and blood of that Jesus who was made flesh.

The Apostles in their memoirs, which are called Gospels, have handed down what Jesus ordered them to do; that He took bread and, after giving thanks, said: "Do this in remembrance of Me; this is my body."

In like manner he took also the chalice, gave thanks, and said: "This is My blood"; and to them only did He give it.

A COMMUNITY OF CHARITY AND PRAYER

c.67 We constantly remind one another of these things. The rich among us come to the aid of the poor, and we always stay together. For all the favors we enjoy we bless the Creator of all, through His Son Jesus Christ and through the Holy Spirit.

CELEBRATION OF THE LORD'S DAY

On the day which is called Sunday we have a common assembly of all who live in the cities or in the outlying districts, and the memoirs of the Apostles or the writings of the Prophets are read, as long as there is time.

Then, when the reader has finished, the president of the assembly verbally admonishes and invites all to imitate such examples of virtue.

Then we rise all together and pray.

As we have already said, as we finish our prayers, bread and wine and water are presented. He who presides likewise offers up prayers and thanksgivings, to the best of his ability, and the people express their approval by saying, "Amen."

The Eucharistic elements are distributed and consumed by those present, and to those who are absent they are sent through the deacons.

The wealthy, if they wish, contribute whatever they desire, and the collection is placed in the custody of the president. [With it] he helps the orphans and widows, those who are needy because of sickness or any other reason, and the captives and strangers in our midst; in short, he takes care of all those in need.

Sunday, indeed, is the day on which we all hold our common assembly because it is the first day on which God, transforming the darkness and matter, created the world; and our Savior Jesus Christ rose from the dead on the same day. For they crucified Him on the day before that of Saturn, and on the day after, which is Sunday, He appeared to His Apostles and disciples, and taught them the things which we have passed on to you also for consideration.

CHAPTER FOUR

THE APOSTOLIC TRADITION OF HIPPOLYTUS

With the exception of The Didache, The Apostolic Tradition *is the earliest and most important of the ancient Church orders which we possess. It is aptly described as a rudimentary "Sacramentary" which sets rules and forms for the hierarchy as well as for the administration of Baptism and the Eucharist. It had been lost for centuries until it was rediscovered and published in 1900 and subsequently shown to be not a derivative of other Church orders as had been thought, but their inspiration. It was long known as the "Egyptian Church Order" for no other reason than that it was known to the modern world in Egyptian and Coptic translations. The present text has been reconstructed from various partial translations in Coptic, Arabic, Ethiopic, and Latin translations, and is in some places conjectural. The translations indicate that it exercised little influence in western Christianity but considerable influence in the East, where it played an important part in the formation of the Eastern liturgy as well as Canon Law.*

Scholars debate the authorship of The Apostolic Tradition. *Some contemporaries continue previous generations' identification of the author as Hippolytus of Rome while others deny that he is the author. However the question is resolved, the document has preserved for us an invaluable portrait of the Church at Rome in its formative years, at the time of Hippolytus.*

The Apostolic Tradition, *which is usually given the date c. 215 for its composition, bears striking resemblance to Jewish forms of worship, for example, in the interrogation about motives before baptism, the manner of anointing the baptized, the long grace or* **berakah** *over the bread and wine, and the introduction to the responsive grace over the final "cup of blessing." Of primary importance is the full account of features of the Eucharistic Liturgy, and the Eucharistic Prayer in particular, which served as the inspiration of present-day Roman Catholicism's Eucharist Prayer II. Also to be noted*

21

are the regulations concerning the rigorous selection process preceding admission to the catechumenate, and the training and discipline of candidates from the time of their admission to the catechumenate, which ordinarily lasted for three years, to the time of their initiation. These aspects emphasize the seriousness with which the early Church looked upon initiation as a mature act of an adult responding to the call to conversion. The rite of initiation is described in considerable detail. A separate form for the celebration of an "agape" is included, which indicates that by the time of Hippolytus and probably for decades prior to his description of the "apostolic tradition," this community meal had become separated from the celebration of the Eucharist.

Scholars recognize a relationship of **The Apostolic Tradition** *to two of the most ancient paschal homilies, those of Melito of Sardis and Pseudo-Hippolytus, based upon similar titles attributed to Jesus, typological expressions, and scriptural citations.*

In the selections from **The Apostolic Tradition** *given here, the original order has been changed in order to present the material relevant to initiation in the order of Baptism, Confirmation, and Eucharist.*

[Translation: Deiss, pp. 52–64, 37–41, 43–47]

THE APOSTOLIC TRADITION OF HIPPOLYTUS

CHRISTIAN INITIATION

[The Admission of Catechumens]

Those who are to be initiated into the new faith must first be brought to the catechists to hear the word, before the people arrive.

They are to be asked their reasons for seeking the faith.

Those who introduce them will bear witness in their regard in order that it may be known whether they are capable of hearing the Word. Their state of life also is to be scrutinized.

Inquiry is to be made about the trades and professions of those who are brought for instruction.

If a man is a procurer, that is to say, supports prostitutes, let him give it up or be sent away.

If he is a sculptor or painter, he is to be instructed not to make any more idols. Let him give it up or be sent away.

If he is an actor or gives performances in the theater, let him give it up or be sent away.

If he teaches children, it is preferable that he should give it up. But if he has no trade, he is to be allowed to continue.

If he is a charioteer, a wrestler or attends wrestling matches, let him give it up or be sent away.

If he is gladiator, or teaches gladiators to fight, or a hunter, or if he is a public official who organizes the gladiatorial games, let him give it up or be sent away.

If he is a priest of idols or a guardian of idols, let him give it up or be sent away.

A soldier who is in a position of authority is not to be allowed to put anyone to death; if he is ordered to, he is not to do it, he is not to be allowed to take an oath. If he does not accept these conditions, he is to be sent away.

A man who has the power of the sword, or magistrate of a city who wears the purple; let him give it up or be sent away.

Catechumens or believers who want to enlist as soldiers are to be sent away, for they have treated God with contempt.

A prostitute, or a pederast, or a man who has mutilated himself, or one who has committed an unspeakable thing, are to be sent away, for they are defiled.

Wizards too are not to be admitted to the interrogation.

Sorcerers, astrologers, fortune-tellers, interpreters of dreams, charlatans, those who pare coins, makers of amulets must give up these activities: otherwise they are to be sent away.

If a concubine who is the slave of some man has brought up her children and is living only with this man, she is to be admitted; otherwise she is to be sent away.

A man who has a concubine is to give her up and take a wife according to the law. If he refuses he is to be sent away.

If we have omitted anything, make a suitable decision yourselves. For we all have the Spirit of God.

[The Three Year Catechumenate]

The catechumen is to attend the instruction for three years.

However, if a man shows himself zealous and really perseveres in this undertaking, you are to judge him not by length of time but by his conduct.

[The Instruction]

When the catechist has finished his instruction, the catechumens are to pray by themselves, apart from the faithful, and the women are to stand praying in some place in the Church apart, whether they are baptized or catechumens.

After the prayer, the catechist is to lay hands on them while he says a prayer and dismisses them. Whether he is of the clergy or the laity, he is to do this.

[Baptism of Blood]

If a catechumen is thrown into prison for the name of God, he is not to be left in doubt as to his witness. For indeed, if he suffers violence and is put to death before he has received pardon for his sins, he will be justified nevertheless, for he is baptized in his own blood.

PREPARATORY RITES FOR BAPTISM

[Choosing the Candidates]

When those who are to be baptized have been chosen, their life is to be examined—whether they have lived devoutly during their catechumenate, whether they have respected widows, visited the sick, practiced all the other good works.

[The Giving of the Gospel]

If those who introduce them bear witness that they have been living in this way, let them hear the Gospel.

[The Daily Exorcisms; the Scrutiny]

From the moment when they have been set apart, they are to undergo exorcisms every day by the imposition of hands.

As the day of their baptism approaches, the bishop is to exorcize each of them, to find out if they are pure. If there is one among them who is not, he is to be rejected, for he has not heard the Word with faith, because it is impossible for the Stranger [demon] to remain always hidden. . . .

[Fasting and Prayer]

Those who are to be baptized must fast on the Friday and Saturday.

On the Saturday, the bishop gathers them all together in one place and bids them all pray and kneel.

As he lays his hands on them, let him conjure all the foreign spirits to depart from them and never to return to them again. When he has finished the exorcism, let him breathe upon their faces, make the sign on their forehead, ears and nose and then bid them rise.

[The Baptismal Vigil]

They are to keep watch through the night. They are to be given readings and instructions.

Those to be baptized are to bring nothing with them other than what they must bring for the Eucharist, for it is fitting that he who has been made worthy of it should make the offering.

[Conferral of Baptism]

At cockcrow, they are to come to the water; this must be running water and pure. . . .

They are to take off their clothes.

The children are baptized first. All those who can, are to reply for themselves. If they cannot, let their parents reply for them, or another member of the family.

Next you baptize the men, then the women; the women will have unbound their hair and taken off their jewels of gold and silver.

No one is to go down into the water with anything of the Stranger.

[The Oil of Thanksgiving and the Oil of Exorcism]

At the time appointed for the baptism, the bishop says a prayer of thanksgiving over the oil and collects it in a vessel. It is this oil which is called "oil of thanksgiving."

Next he takes another oil and pronounces an exorcism over it; this oil is called "oil of exorcism."

The deacon carries the oil of exorcism and stands on the left of the priest. Another deacon takes the oil of thanksgiving and stands on the right of the priest.

[Renunciation of Satan]

The priest takes each of those who are to receive baptism aside. He orders each to renounce in these terms:

I renounce you, Satan,
and all your undertakings
and all your works.

[The Anointing of Exorcism]

After this renunciation, he gives them an anointing with the oil of exorcism, saying:

Let every evil spirit depart from you.

Then he leads them back to the bishop or to the priest, who is standing near the water to baptize.

[The Triple Immersion]

The deacon is to go down with him [into the water]. He who is baptizing him lays his hand on his head and asks him:

Do you believe in God, the almighty Father?

The one who is being baptized replies:

"I believe."

Then he baptizes him the first time, keeping his hand laid on his head.

Next he asks him:

> Do you believe in Christ Jesus,
> the Son of God,
> born by the Holy Spirit of the Virgin Mary,
> who was crucified under Pontius Pilate,
> who died and was buried,
> who rose again on the third day,
> living from among the dead,
> who ascended into heaven,
> who sits at the right hand of the Father,
> who will come to judge the living and the dead?

When he replies: "I believe," he baptizes him a second time.

He asks him again:

> Do you believe in the Holy Spirit,
> in the Holy Church,
> and in the resurrection of the flesh?

He who is being baptized replies: "I believe."
Then he is baptized a third time.

[The Anointing with the Oil of Thanksgiving]

After that he comes up again. Then the priest gives him an anointing with the oil which has been sanctified. He says:

> I anoint you with the holy oil in the name of Jesus Christ.

After they have dried themselves, they put on their clothes again and go into the church.

[THE GIFT OF THE SPIRIT]

[The Laying on of Hands]

> As he lays his hands on them, the bishop invokes (God) saying:
> Lord God,
> who have given to these the
> dignity of meriting the remission
> of their sins through the bath of

regeneration to make them worthy
to be filled with the Holy Spirit,
fill them with your grace that they
may serve you according to your will.

For to you is the glory,
Father and Son, with the Holy Spirit
in the holy Church,
now and for ever and ever. Amen.

[The Anointing]

Next, from his hand, he pours out the blessed oil. He puts it on their heads saying:

I give you the anointing with the blessed oil,
in the Lord God, the almighty Father,
Christ Jesus and the Holy Spirit.

[The Seal]

Next he marks them with the sign on the forehead, then he gives them a kiss saying:

The Lord is with you.

He who has been marked with the sign replies:

And with your spirit.

This is to be done for each of them. From then on they are to pray with the whole people. But they are not to pray with the faithful until they have received all this.

When they have prayed, let them give the kiss of peace.

THE BAPTISMAL MASS AND FIRST COMMUNION

[The Offering]

The deacons present the offering to the bishop.
He blesses the bread which represents the body of Christ; the chalice in which the wine is mixed, which represents the blood poured out for all those who believe in him; the milk and honey

mixed together, to signify the fulfillment of the promise which was made to our fathers, signified by the land flowing with milk and honey, realized by the flesh of Christ which he gives us, by which the believers are nourished like little children, for the sweetness of his word changes the bitterness of our hearts to gentleness; lastly, the water for the offering to signify purification, so that the inward man who is spiritual may receive the same effect as the body. The bishop explains all this to those who receive communion.

[Communion]

Having broken the bread, he distributes each morsel saying:

"The bread of heaven in Christ Jesus."

He who receives it replies: "Amen."

And those who receive taste from each of the chalices, while the minister says three times:

"In God the almighty Father,
and in the Lord Christ,
and in the Holy Spirit
and in the Holy Church."

He replies: "Amen." This is to be done for each of them.

When this is finished, each hastens to do good works, to please God and to live a good life. He is to devote himself to the Church, putting what he has been taught into practice and making progress in the service of God.

THE AGAPE

When the bishop eats with the rest of the faithful, each receives a morsel of bread from his hand before breaking his own. This is "blessed bread" and not the Eucharist like the body of the Lord.

Before drinking, each should take a cup and give thanks over it. Then you may eat and drink, after you have been purified in this way....

COMMUNION IN THE HOME

Every believer, before tasting other food, is to take care to receive the Eucharist. For if he receives it with faith, even if he is given some deadly poison, it will not be able to do him harm.

Everyone is to take care that no unbaptised person, no mouse, or other animal eats of the Eucharist, and that no particle of the Eucharist falls on the ground or is lost. For it is the body of Christ to be eaten by the faithful and not to be treated carelessly.

THE EUCHARISTIC PRAYER AT AN EPISCOPAL ORDINATION

[Acclamation]

When he has been consecrated bishop, let all give him the kiss of peace and greet him because he has been made worthy.

Let the deacons present the offering to him. When he lays his hands on it, with the whole college of priests, let him say the words of thanksgiving:

Bishop:	The Lord be with you.
People:	And with your spirit.
Bishop:	Let us lift up our hearts.
People:	They are turned to the Lord.
Bishop:	Let us give thanks to the Lord.
People:	It is worthy and just.

[Thanksgiving]

Let him then continue thus:

We give you thanks, O God,
through thy beloved Child, Jesus Christ,
whom you have sent to us in the last times
as Savior, Redeemer and Messenger of your will.
He is your inseparable Word
through whom you have created all things
and in whom you were well pleased.
You sent him from heaven
into the womb of a Virgin

He was conceived and became incarnate,
and was manifested as your Son,
born of the Holy Spirit and the Virgin.
He accomplished your will
and, to acquire a holy people for you,
he stretched out his hands while he suffered
to deliver from suffering
those who have believed in you.

[Account of the Institution]

When he gave himself up willingly to suffering
to destroy death,
to break the fetters of the devil,
to trample hell under his feet,
to spread his light over the just,
to establish the limit
and manifest his Resurrection,
he took bread,
he gave you thanks and said:

"Take, eat, this is my body,
which will be broken for you."

Likewise for the chalice, he said:

"This is my blood
which is poured out for you.
When you do this,
do it in memory of me."

[Anamnesis]

We then, remembering his death
and his Resurrection,
offer you bread and wine,
we give you thanks for having judged us worthy
to stand before you and serve you.

[Epiclesis]

> And we beg you
> to send your Holy Spirit
> upon the offering of your holy Church.
> Gathering and uniting all those who receive it,
> grant that they be filled with the Holy Spirit
> for the strengthening of their faith in the truth.
> So may we be able to praise and glorify you
> through your Son Jesus Christ.

[Doxology]

> Through him, glory to you, and honor,
> to the Father and to the Son, with the Holy Spirit,
> in your holy Church, now and for ever. Amen.

[The rest of the liturgy is probably a later addition.]

CHAPTER FIVE

THE ANAPHORA OF ADDAI AND MARI

*The Anaphora of "The Apostles," Addai and Mari, traditional founders of Edessa, in northeast Syria, is among the oldest surviving Eucharistic Prayers. It is still in use among Nestorians as well as Uniate Chaldeans and Christians of Malabar in southern India. Some scholars believe that in its original form it is to be dated as early as the third century, from about the same period as **The Apostolic Tradition** of Hippolytus. Others believe that it is no earlier than the fifth century. The recent discovery of a manuscript some five centuries older than the sixteenth century version which scholars previously studied has renewed interest in it. Composed in Syriac (an Aramaic dialect), it preserves, once later additions are deleted, the Eucharistic Prayer of the ancient church of Edessa. Because Edessa, one of the earliest centers of Christianity, was situated outside the frontiers of the Roman Empire, it was less subject to the developments which took place in Greek-speaking Christendom. As a result, the anaphora preserves to a greater degree than others the semitic structure, style, and content of the Jewish table blessings, the **berakoth**. There is general agreement among scholars that the introductory dialogue and the "Sanctus" are later additions, although they may have been added quite early. It is also possible that the **epiclesis** and the interecessions are later additions as well. It appears that this anaphora and that known as the **Sharar** or "The Third Anaphora of St. Peter" share a common ancestry but developed in different ways. Given their relatedness, it is difficult to explain why that of Addai and Mari contains no narrative of the Institution but does have an **anamnesis**, while the **Sharar** has a narrative of institution but no **anamnesis**. It is possible that **the anaphora** of Addai and Mari once had an account of the institution but that it was dropped before the tenth century. The Uniate Chaldeans have placed the account where it is indicated in the translation given below, just prior to the **anamnesis**. The **epiclesis** represents an early stage of development and is similar to that found in **The Apostolic Tradition**.*

*Common to both is the invocation of the Holy Spirit upon the gifts and assembly, but there is no specific petition that the Spirit transform the offerings so that they may become the Body and Blood of the Lord. An additional difficulty which confronts commentators may be noted. The prayer begins by addressing the Trinity and concludes by addressing the Father, while the **anamnesis**, which is central, is addressed first to the Son and then to the Father. The original prayer, transmitted orally before it was committed to writing and expanded by later additions, is beautiful in its simplicity.*
[Translation: Deiss, pp. 137–141]

THE ANAPHORA OF ADDAI AND MARI

[Acclamation]

> The grace of our Lord Jesus Christ,
> the love of God the Father
> and the fellowship of the Holy Spirit
> be with us all
> now and always
> and for ever and ever.
> Amen.
>
> Lift up your hearts.
> To thee, King of glory, God of Abraham, Issac and Jacob.
> The oblation is offered to God,
> To the Lord of the universe.
> It is worthy and necessary.

[Preface]

> It is worthy that all mouths glorify,
> that all tongues proclaim,
> that all creatures adore and magnify
> the adorable name of the glorious Trinity,
> of the Father, Son, and Holy Spirit.
> He has created the world through his grace,
> and in his kindness those who dwell in it.
> He has saved men in his mercy,
> He has granted to mortals the riches of his grace.

[Sanctus]

Thousand upon thousands of heavenly spirits
bless thee and adore thy majesty.
Myriads upon myriads of the holy angels of the
army of spiritual beings,
of servants of fire and spirit
sing thy name.
With the holy Cherubim and the spiritual Seraphim
they glorify and adore thy greatness.
They call ceaselessly
and reply one to another:

Holy, holy, holy is the Lord God Sabaoth!
Heaven and earth are filled
with his splendor, his presence
and the brilliance of his glorious light.
Hosanna to the highest heaven!
Hosanna to the son of David!
Blessed be he who comes and is to come
in the name of the Lord.
Hosanna to the highest heaven!
And with the heavenly powers.

[Preface (continued)]

We also bless thee, Lord,
We thy servants, weak, feeble and frail,
for the measureless grace that thou has done us
for which we cannot repay thee.

Thou hast clothed thyself in our humanity,
to give us life through thy godhead.
Thou has lifted up our lowliness,
thou hast restored our fall.
Thou has raised up our mortality,
thou hast forgiven our faults,
thou has justified us out of our sins.
Thou has enlightened our understanding.
Thou hast condemned our enemies, Lord our God,

Thou has given triumph
to the frailty of our feeble nature,
Through the abundant mercies of thy grace.
For all thy help and thy grace
we offer thee praise and blessing,
honor and adoration,
now and always
and for ever and ever.
Amen.

[THE ACCOUNT OF THE INSTITUTION]

[Anamnesis]

Lord, through thy many mercies
which cannot be told, be graciously
mindful of all the pious and righteous
Fathers who were pleasing in thy sight,
in the commemoration of the body and blood
of thy Christ, which we offer to thee
on the pure and holy altar,
as you taught us.

And we too, Lord, thy servants,
weak, feeble and frail,
who are gathered in thy name,
we stand before thee at this time,
we have received from tradition
the form which comes from thee.

With joy and exultation,
we give glory to thee,
we commemorate and accomplish
this great, fearful and holy,
life-giving and divine mystery
of the passion and the death,
the burial and the resurrection
of our Lord and our Savior Jesus Christ.

[Epiclesis]

> Let thy Holy Spirit, Lord, come
> and rest upon this offering of thy servants,
> let him bless it and sanctify it,
> so that it may procure for us, Lord,
> pardon for our offences and forgiveness of our sins,
> the great hope of the resurrection of the dead,
> and the new life in the kingdom of heaven
> with all those who were pleasing to thee.

[Final Doxology]

> For thy great and wonderful design
> that thou has realized in our regard,
> let us bless thee and glorify thee without end
> in thy Church that thou hast redeemed
> with the precious blood of thy Christ.
> With open mouths and faces uncovered
> we offer praise and glory,
> blessing and adoration
> to thy living, holy and life-giving name,
> now and always,
> and for ever and ever.
> Amen.

CHAPTER SIX

THE EUCHOLOGION OF SERAPION

*The Euchologion (Prayer Book) of Serapion, Bishop of Thumis, a small region in Lower Egypt, in the middle of the fourth century, was discovered in 1894 on Mt. Athos. Little is known of his life other than that as a young man he had retired to the desert where he was one of St. Anthony's favorite disciples. He was also a friend of St. Athanasius of Alexandria and undertook his defense against charges brought by the Arians before the Emperor Constantine. Since Athanasius' correspondence with him took place prior to 362, his death took place after that date. Serapion's Prayer Book contains thirty liturgical prayers. The most important of these is **The Anaphora** and then the prayers accompanying the liturgies of baptism. Serapion made use of existing texts and modified them. The prayer following the first part of the Institution Narrative unquestionably depends upon **The Didache**. Of particular interest is the surprising invocation in the **epiclesis** of the Word rather than the customary invocation of the Holy Spirit to bring about the change in the elements of bread and wine. There are other examples in **The Euchology** of invoking the sanctifying power of the Word, particularly in the prayers accompanying the rites of initiation. It is also at least possible, if not probable, that Serapion is thereby asserting in solemn prayer the orthodox faith against Arianism. (Some scholars, however, find Arian elements in the text, which make them reluctant to accept without qualification that Serapion was the author.) There is a tenderness to Serapion's prayers, revealed in his repeated appeals to the love of God for his people, and a confidence in that love which shines through again and again.*
[Translation: Deiss, pp. 113–118, 122–129]

THE EUCHOLOGION OF SERAPION

THE EUCHARISTIC LITURGY

Prayer of the Anaphora

[Preface]

It is worthy and just to praise you,
to celebrate you, to glorify you,
uncreated Father of the only-begotten Son,
Jesus Christ.

We praise you, uncreated God,
inscrutable, indescribable,
incomprehensible to every created nature.

We praise you, you who are known to the Only-begotten
Son, you of whom he spoke, whom he interpreted,
whom he made known to created nature.

We praise you, you who know the Son
and reveal his glory to the holy,
you who are known to the Word
whom you have begotten,
and have been interpreted to the holy.

We praise you, invisible Father
who give immortality.
You are the source of life, the source of light,
the source of all grace and all truth.
You love men, you love the poor,
you reconcile yourself with all,
you draw all to yourself
through the coming of your beloved Son.

We pray you, make of us living men.
Give us the Spirit of light
"that we may know you, you the True
and him whom you have sent, Jesus Christ."

Give us Holy Spirit that we may be able
to proclaim and tell forth indescribable mysteries!
May the Lord Jesus speak in us and also Holy Spirit,
and may he celebrate you with hymns through us!

For you are above every Principality,
Power, Virtue and Domination,
above every name that is named
in this age as in the age to come.

You are attended by thousands upon thousands
and myriads upon myriads
of Angels and Archangels,
of Thrones and Dominions,
of Principalities and Powers.
Beside you stand
the two august Seraphim with six wings:
two to cover the face,
two to cover the feet,
two with which to fly.
They sing your holiness.
With theirs, accept also
our acclamation of your holiness:

[Sanctus]

Holy, holy, holy, is the Lord Sabaoth!
Heaven and earth are filled with your glory.
The heaven is filled, the earth is filled
with your wonderful glory!

[The Account of the Institution]

Lord of powers,
fill this sacrifice too
with your power and your participation.
It is to you that we have offered
this living sacrifice, this bloodless offering.
It is to you that we have offered this bread,
figure of the body of the Only begotten.
This bread is the figure of the holy body.

For the Lord Jesus Christ, the night when he was
betrayed, took bread, broke it
and gave it to his disciples saying:
"Take and eat, this is my body,
which is broken for you
for the remission of sins."

For this reason, we too,
celebrating the figure of his death,
have offered the bread and pray,
through this sacrifice to be reconciled to all of us;
be favorable to us, O God of truth.
And just as this bread,
once scattered upon the hills,
has been gathered together to become one,
so too, deign to reunite your holy Church
from every people, from every land,
from every town, village and house,
and make her one living and Catholic Church.

We have offered too the cup, figure of the blood.
For the Lord Jesus Christ, after the supper,
took the cup and said to his disciples:
"Take and drink,
this is the New Covenant,
that is, my blood poured out for you
for the remission of sins."
For this reason we too have offered
the cup, presenting the figure of the blood.

[Invocation of the Word]

O God of truth,
may your holy Word come down upon this bread,
that it may become the body of the Word,
and upon this cup,
that it may become the blood of the Truth.
Grant that all who communicate
may receive a life-giving remedy,
which may heal every infirmity in them,

which may strengthen them for all progress and virtue,
let it not be a cause, O God of truth,
of condemnation, accusation or shame.

[Memento of the Living]

For we have called on you, the Uncreated God,
through your Only-begotten Son, in Holy Spirit:
Take pity on this people,
judge them worthy of progress.
Send your Angels to be with this people,
to help them triumph over the Evil One
and to strengthen your Church.

[Memento of the Dead]

We pray too for all
who have fallen asleep.
whom we call to mind.

[After recalling the names]

Sanctify these souls,
for you know them all.
Sanctify all those who have fallen asleep in the Lord.
Number them all with your holy Powers
give them a place and a dwelling in your Kingdom.

[Final Prayer and doxology]

Accept also the thanksgiving of your people.
Bless those who have presented to you
these offerings and thanksgivings.
Give all this people health,
prosperity and happiness,
all that advances the welfare of soul and body.

Through your Only-begotten, Jesus Christ,
in Holy Spirit,
as it was, and is and will be,
from generation to generation
and for ever and ever. Amen.

[Prayer at the Breaking of the Bread]

Make us worthy too of this communion,
O God of truth,
and grant that our bodies may receive in purity,
our souls understanding and knowledge.
Give us wisdom, O God of mercies,
through sharing the body and blood.

Glory to you and power,
through the Only begotten,
in Holy Spirit,
now and forever and ever. Amen.

[Blessing of the People after the Breaking of the Bread]

I lift my hand over this people
and I pray you to stretch out the hand of truth
and to bless this people here, in the name of
your love for men, O God of mercies,
and in the name of the mysteries
which we celebrate.

Let the hand of discretion and power,
the hand of wisdom, purity and all holiness
bless this people and keep them
so that they may progress and be improved,
Through your Only-begotten, Jesus Christ,
in Holy Spirit,
now and for ever and ever. Amen.

[Prayer after the Communion of the People]

We give you thanks, O Master,
for having called those who were in error,
for having reconciled those who had sinned.
You have over-looked the threat which weighed on us,
through your love for men, you have withdrawn it,
through conversion, you have wiped it away,
through your knowledge you have rejected it.

We give you thanks
for having made us "to participate in the body and the
blood." Bless us and bless this people.
Grant us to have a share with the body and blood.

Through your Only-begotten Son.
Through him, glory to you and power,
in Holy Spirit,
now and for ever and ever. Amen.

THE RITES OF INITIATION

[Consecration of the Baptismal Waters]

King and Lord of all things,
Creator of the Universe:
Through the descent of your Only-begotten Jesus Christ,
you have given to all created nature
the grace of salvation;
you have redeemed your creation
by the coming of your unutterable Word.
Look down now from the height of heaven,
cast your eyes on these waters,
fill them with Holy Spirit.

Let your unutterable Word be in them,
let him transform their power.
Let him give them the power to be fertile,
let him fill them with your grace,
so that the mystery which is now being accomplished
may not prove fruitless in those who are going to be
regenerated but may fill with your divine grace
all those who go down (into the baptismal font)
and are baptized.

You love men, O benefactor,
take pity on those you created,
save your creation, the work of your right hand.
Transfigure all those who are going to be reborn
with your divine and unspeakable form.

Transfigured and regenerated,
let them be thus saved,
"be judged worthy of your Kingdom" (2 Thes 1,5).
Just as the Word, your Only-begotten,
by descending upon the waters of the Jordan,
conferred sanctification on them,
even so let him descend now upon these waters
to render them holy and spiritual,
so that the baptized
may no longer be "flesh and blood,"
but may become "spiritual,"
and may be able to adore you, the eternal Father,
through Jesus Christ, in Holy Spirit.

Through him, glory to you and power
for ever and ever. Amen.

[Prayer of Exorcism]

We pray you, God of truth,
for your servant who is here.
We beg you to make him worthy
of the divine mystery and your unutterable regeneration,
for it is to you who love men
that we offer him.
It is to thee that we consecrate him.

According to your grace, let him share in this regeneration,
let him no longer be under the influence
of any evil and wicked spirit;
but let him serve you at all times,
let him keep your commandments,
as your Only-begotten Word guides him.

Through him glory to thee and power,
in Holy Spirit,
now and for ever and ever. Amen.

[Prayer after the Renunciation]

Almighty Lord, seal with your approval

the assent which your servant here
has now given you.

Keep firm his moral life and his conduct.
Let him no longer henceforth be the slave of evil,
but serve the God of truth.

Let him submit himself,
to you, the Creator of the universe,
and show himself a perfect and true son.

Through your Only-begotten, Jesus Christ.
Through him glory to you and power,
in Holy Spirit,
now and forever and ever. Amen.

[Prayer for the Oil for the Anointing of the Catechumens]

O Master, you who love men
and who love souls,
God of mercy, pity and truth,
we call on you following out and obeying
the promises of your Only-begotten
who said, "Those whose sins you shall forgive,
they shall be forgiven them."

We anoint with this oil these men and women
who present themselves for this
divine regeneration.

We beseech our Lord Jesus Christ
to give them the power which heals and strengthens.

Let him manifest himself through this anointing,
let him remove from their souls,
from their bodies or their spirits,
every sign of sin, of iniquity
or diabolic blame.

Let him through his own grace,
grant them forgiveness.

Freed from sin,
let them live for righteousness.

Now that they have become a new creation through
this anointing, purified by this bath and renewed in
spirit, let them have the power to overcome
henceforth all the forces of the enemy
which are ranged against them,
and all the deceits of this life.
Let them be gathered and reunited to the flock
of our Lord and Savior Jesus Christ.

Let them share with the saints
the promised inheritance.

Through him, glory to you and power,
in Holy Spirit,
for ever and ever. Amen.

[Prayer after the Anointing]

You who love men, Benefactor,
Savior of all who have turned to you:

Be gracious to this servant here;
let your right hand lead him to regeneration.
Let your Only-begotten Word,
draw him to the [baptismal] font.

Let his new birth be honored,
let your grace not be fruitless.

Let your holy Word be beside him,
Let your Holy Spirit be with him,
let him repel and put to flight every temptation,

Through your Only-begotten, Jesus Christ,
glory to you and power,
in Holy Spirit,
now and forever and ever. Amen.

[Prayer for the Neophytes]

God, God of truth, Creator of the universe,
and Lord of all creation,
richly endow your servant here with your blessing.
Make him to share in the angelic powers,
so that henceforth he, who has had a part
in your divine and profitable gift,
may be named no longer flesh but spiritual.
Keep him, to the very end, for yourself,
Creator of all things.

Through your Only-begotten, Jesus Christ,
Through him, glory to you and power,
in Holy Spirit,
now and for ever and ever. Amen.

ANOINTING AFTER BAPTISM

[Prayer for the Chrism with which the Baptized are Anointed]

God of the [heavenly] powers,
help of every soul who turns to you
and who places himself under the powerful hand
of your Only-begotten, we call on you:
By the divine and invisible power
of our Lord and Savior Jesus Christ,
carry out through this oil
thy divine and heavenly work.

May those who have been baptized and received the
anointing, with the impress of the sign
of the saving cross of the Only-begotten,
by which cross Satan and every hostile power have
been defeated and are led captive
in the triumphal procession.

Regenerated and renewed
by the bath of new birth,
may these here also share
in the gifts of Holy Spirit.

Strengthened by the seal,
let them remain "steadfast and immovable" (1 Cor 15,58),
sheltered from all attack and pillaging,
subjected neither to insult nor intrigue.

Let them remain to the very end
living in the faith and knowledge of the truth,
in the expectation of the hope of heavenly life
and of the eternal promises
of our Lord and Savior, Jesus Christ.

Through him, glory to thee and power,
in Holy Spirit,
now and for ever and ever. Amen.

CHAPTER SEVEN

THE APOSTOLIC CONSTITUTIONS

The Apostolic Constitutions were compiled in the latter part of the fourth century (it cannot be earlier since it mentions the celebration of Christmas which was not introduced into the East before this time) and all indications are that it is of Syro-Palestinian origin. It represents the largest liturgical-canonical collection of the ancient church. Although it purports to give the decrees which Pope Clement of Rome received from the Apostles, it is in fact apocryphal. The compiler has made use of existing texts and ascribed them to Pope Clement I, a disciple of the Apostles, in order to give them the weight and authority of a revered leader of the primitive Church. Three existing documents have been used: The Didache is included in expanded form in Book VII, the Didascalia of the Apostles is the source of Books I–VI, and Book VIII follows in a rather free way, the outline of The Apostolic Tradition of Hippolytus. The orthodoxy of the compiler was suspect from an early date. Because of expressions which appeared tinged with Arianism, the document was condemned at the Trullan Synod (692). Such expressions in a document which was long thought to be of apostolic origin were explained as falsifications introduced into the text by heretics. These expressions, however, were probably always contained in the documents. It appears most likely that, as a whole, the liturgy of The Apostolic Constitutions was never used. Nonetheless, it is also quite certain that one or another part of it had been or still was in use in some of the early Eastern Churches. Selections from the whole which appear here are from the euchology (prayer book) of Book VII and the Eucharistic Liturgy, the so-called "Clementine" liturgy of Book VIII. Of particular interest in the former is the prayer accompanying the anointing rite which the later Church would term "confirmation," although here it is not linked with the gift of the Spirit. Book VIII contains the liturgy of the catechumens, which followed upon the readings, up to the point when the catechumens and penitents were dismissed from the assembly. Of even greater interest is the liturgy which follows. The prayer of the faithful is characterized by a breadth of tender concern for those within and outside the Church. The Eucharistic Prayer contains traces of Hippolytus' **Apostolic Tradition** *within the* **anamnesis** *and* **epiclesis.** *However, the liturgy is the creation of the editor and appears not to have been intended as a formulary to be followed but rather as a source from which a celebrant could freely draw in composing his own prayer. The outline suggested would soon be adopted by the great bishop of Antioch, John Chrysostom. The Apostolic Constitutions are an important witness to the liturgy of the fourth century. The first selection is from Book VII, the remainder from Book VIII.*

[Translation: Constitutions concerning Baptism, ANF, pp. 431, 476–477; Liturgies, Deiss, pp. 152, 157–158, 161–164, 169–174, 178–183]

THE APOSTOLIC CONSTITUTIONS

CONSTITUTIONS CONCERNING BAPTISM

Ordain also a deaconess who is faithful and holy, for the ministrations towards women. For sometimes he [the bishop] cannot send a deacon, who is a man, to the women, on account of unbelievers. You will therefore send a woman, a deaconess, on account of the imaginations of the evil-minded. For we stand in need of a woman, a deaconess, for many necessities; and first in the baptism of women, the deacon shall anoint only their forehead with the holy oil, and after him the deaconess shall anoint them; for there is no necessity that the women should be seen by the men; but only in the laying on of hands the bishop shall anoint her head, as the priest and kings were formerly anointed, not because those who are now baptized are ordained priests, but as being christian, or anointed, from Christ the Anointed, "a royal priesthood, and an holy nation, the Church of God, the pillar and ground of the marriage-chamber" (1 Pet 2.9), who formerly were not a people, but now are beloved and chosen, upon whom is called His new name, as Isaiah the prophet witnesses, saying: "And they shall call the people by His new name, which the Lord shall name for them" (Is 42.2).

Therefore, Bishop, according to that type, you shall anoint the head of those that are to be baptized, whether they be men or women, with the holy oil, for a type of the spiritual baptism. After that, either you, bishop, or a presbyter that is under you, shall in the solemn form name over them the Father, and Son, and Holy Spirit, and shall dip them in the water; and let a deacon receive the man, and a deaconess the woman, that so the conferring of this inviolable seal may take place with a becoming decency. And after that, let the bishop anoint those that are baptized with ointment.

This baptism, therefore, is given into the death of Jesus: the water is instead of burial, and the oil instead of the Holy Spirit; the seal instead of the cross; the ointment is the confirmation of the confession; the mention of the Father as of the Author and Sender; the joint mention of the Holy Spirit as of the witness; the descent into the water the dying together with Christ; the ascent out of the water the rising again with Him. The Father is the God over all; Christ is the Only-begotten God, the beloved Son, the Lord of glory; the Holy Spirit is the Comforter, who is sent by Christ, and taught by Him and proclaims Him.

But let him that is to be baptized be free from all iniquity; one that has left off to work sin, the friend of God, the enemy of the devil, the heir of God the Father, the fellow-heir of His Son; one that has renounced Satan, and the demons, and Satan's deceits; chaste, pure, holy, beloved of God, the son of God, praying as a son to his father, and saying, as from the common congregation of the faithful, thus: "Our Father, who art in heaven, hallowed be thy name; thy Kingdom come, thy will be done on earth, as it is in heaven; give us this day our daily bread; and forgive us our trespasses, as we forgive those who trespass against us; and lead us not into temptation, but deliver us from the evil one; for thine is the kingdom, and the power, and the glory, for ever. Amen."

[Renunciation of Satan and Allegiance to Christ]

And when it remains that the catechumen is to be baptized, let him learn what concerns the renunciation of the devil, and the joining himself with Christ; for it is fit that he should first abstain from things contrary, and then be admitted to the mysteries. He must beforehand, purify his heart from all wickedness of disposition, from all spot and wrinkle, and then partake of the holy things; for as the most skilled husbandman does first purge his ground of the thorns which are grown up therein, and does then sow his wheat, so ought you also to take away all impiety from them, and then to sow the seeds of piety in them, and vouchsafe them baptism. . . . Let therefore, the candidate for baptism declare thus in his renunciation:

"I renounce Satan and his works, and his pomps, and his worships, and his angels, and his inventions, and all things that are under him." And after his renunciation let him in his consociation say: "And I associate myself to Christ, and believe, and am baptized into one unbegotten Being, the only true God Almighty, the Father of Christ, the Creator and Maker of all things, from whom are all things; and into the Lord Jesus Christ, His only begotten Son, the First-born of the whole creation, who before the ages was begotten by the good pleasure of the Father, by whom all things were made, both those in heaven and those on earth, visible and invisible; who in the last days descended from heaven, and took flesh, and was born of the Virgin Mary, and did converse holily according to the laws of His God and Father, and was crucified under Pontius Pilate, and died for us, and rose again from the dead after His passion the third day, and ascended into the heavens, and sitteth at the right hand of the Father, and again is to come at the end of the world with glory to judge the quick and the dead, of whose kingdom there shall be no end. And I am baptized into the Holy Spirit, that is the Comforter, who wrought in all the saints from the beginning of the world, but was afterwards sent to the apostles by the Father, according to the promise of our Saviour and Lord, Jesus Christ; and after the apostles, to all those that believe in the Holy Catholic Church; into the resurrection of the flesh and into the remission of sins, and into the kingdom of heaven, and into the life of the world to come." And after this vow, he comes in order to the anointing with oil.

[Blessing of the Oil]

Now this is blessed by the high priest [bishop] for the remission of sins, and the first preparation for baptism. For he calls thus upon the unbegotten God, the Father of Christ, the King of all sensible and intelligible natures, that He would sanctify the oil in the name of the Lord Jesus, and impart to it spiritual grace and efficacious strength, the remission of sins, and the first preparation for the confession of baptism, so that the candidate for baptism, when he is anointed, may be free from all ungodliness, and may become worthy of initiation, according to the command of the Only-begotten.

[Blessing of the Water]

Him, therefore, let the priest even now call upon in baptism, and let him say: "Look down from heaven, and sanctify this water, and give it grace and power, that so he that is to be baptized, according to the command of thy Christ, may be crucified with Him and may die with Him, and may be buried with Him, and may rise with Him to the adoption which is in Him, that he may be dead to sin and live to righteousness."

ANOINTING AFTER BAPTISM

When the bishop has administered baptism in the name of the Father, and of the Son, and of the Holy Spirit, he gives the [neophyte] an anointing with chrism. He is to say:

Lord God, unbegotten and without a superior,
Lord of all things,
who has diffused among all nations
the sweet fragrance of the knowledge of the Gospel:
let this chrism be effective for the one baptized;
through it, let the fragrance of Christ
abide in him firm and stable;
let it raise and give life
to him who has died with Christ. . . .

[The Our Father]

After that, [the neophyte] is to stand up and say the prayer the Lord taught us.

[Ritual of Prayer]

It is right that he who is risen should stand upright to pray, for when one is risen one stands upright. He who has died and risen with Christ is therefore to stand upright.

He is to turn to the East when he prays. For this is written in the second book of Chronicles: when Solomon had finished building the temple of the Lord, at the Dedication, the priests, the levites and the singers, with cymbals and harps, turned to the East, praising, blessing and singing:

Praise the Lord, for he is good,
for his mercy is everlasting (2 Chron 5.12–13).

[Prayer of the One Confirmed]

After the first prayer, he is to say:

Almighty God,
Father of your Christ, your only begotten Son,
give me a spotless body, a clean heart,
a watchful spirit, a knowledge without error.
Let the Holy Spirit come
so that I may possess the truth and believe it firmly,
through your Christ.

By him, glory to you, in the Holy Spirit,
for ever. Amen.

THE LITURGY OF THE MASS

THE LITURGY OF THE CATECHUMENS

[Litany for the Catechumens]

Let the deacon say: "Catechumens, pray."

Let all the faithful then pray for them whole heartedly saying:

"Kyrie Eleison." Let the deacon pray for them like this:

Let us all pray fervently to God for the catechumens.

May he who is good and who loves men listen graciously to their prayers and supplications, may he accede to their requests and give them his help, may he grant the desire of their heart, for their good.

May he reveal the Gospel of Christ to them, may he give them light and understanding, may he instruct them in divine knowledge.

May he teach them his laws and his commandments, may he fill them with his pure and salutary fear.

May he open the ears of their heart, so that they may meditate on his law day and night.

May he strengthen them in devotion, may he unite and gather them into his holy flock.

May he judge them worthy of the bath of the new birth, of the garment of immortality and of true life.

May he rescue them from all wickedness, may the Adversary be unable to attack them, "may he cleanse them flesh and spirit from all defilement" (2 Cor 7.1).

"May he dwell and walk in the midst of them" (2 Cor 6. 16) through his Christ, "may he bless their coming in and their going out" (Ps 121.8), may he bring all their designs to completion for their good.

Let us again beg fervently that they may obtain forgiveness of their sins and through the initiation [of baptism], become worthy of the holy mysteries and the community of the saints.

Rise, catechumens. Ask peace of God through his Christ: that your day, as well as your life, may be filled with this peace and remain sheltered from sin. [Ask for] a Christian death, for the mercy and kindness of God, for forgiveness of sins. Recommend yourselves to the only unbegotten God, through his Christ. Bow down and receive the blessing.

To all these petitions which the deacon announces, let the people, especially the children, reply "Kyrie Eleison" as we have already said.

[Blessing of the Catechumens]

While the catechumens bow their heads the newly ordained bishop pronounces this blessing over them:

> Almighty God, unbegotten and unapproachable,
> You the only true God,
> God and Father of your Christ, your Only-begotten Son,
> God of the Paraclete and Lord of all things,
> who has appointed your disciples teachers of the
> instruction of truth:
> Cast your eyes now on your servants
> who are being instructed in the Gospel of your Christ.
> Give them "a new heart,
> renew a right spirit in their breast" (Ps 51.12),
> so that they may know you
> and may do your will
> "with their whole heart and willingly" (2 Mac 1.3).
> Make them worthy of the holy initiation,
> join them to your holy Church,
> grant them to share in your divine mysteries,
> through Jesus Christ, our hope,
> who died for them.
> Through him, glory to you and adoration,
> in Holy Spirit, for ever. Amen.

[Dismissal of the Catechumens]

After that, the deacon is to say: "Catechumens, go in peace."

[Litany for the Faithful]

The deacon again says: Let no one come near who does not have the right. Let us all, the faithful, kneel. Let us pray to God through his Christ.

[There follows a lengthy series of petitions in which the community prays for the world, the Church, its various office holders and ministers, benefactors, neophytes, travelers, and children. The deacon then says: "Let us rise. Let us pray fervently for one another and recommend ourselves to the living God through his Christ." The bishop then prays for the members of the community.]

THE CELEBRATION OF THE EUCHARIST

[The Kiss of Peace]

Next the deacon says: Let us all attend.

The bishop then greets the assembly saying: The peace of God be with you all.

The people reply: And with your spirit.

The deacon says to all: Greet one another with a holy kiss.

The clergy then give the kiss [of peace] to the bishop, laymen give it to laymen, and women to women.

THE ANAPHORA

[Acclamation]

The bishop then begins the prayer, standing in front of the altar: he is surrounded by the priests and splendidly vested. With his hand he signs his forehead with the triumphant sign of the cross and says:

"The grace of almighty God, the love of our Lord Jesus Christ and the communion of the Holy Spirit be with you all."

With one voice all reply: "And with your minds."
Then the bishop: "Let us raise our spirits."

All: "They are turned to the Lord."

The bishop: "Let us give thanks to the Lord."

All the assembly: "It is worthy and just."

[Thanksgiving]

The bishop continues: It is worthy and just to praise you first of all, you the one true God who existed before creation, from whom "all fatherhood in heaven and on earth . . ." For all these benefits we give glory to thee, almighty Lord.

[Sanctus]

It is you who are adored by the numberless companies of Angels, Archangels, Thrones, Dominions, Principalities, Powers and Virtues, of the hosts of eternity, as well as the Cherubim and the Seraphim with six wings, two to cover their feet, two to veil the head and two with which to fly. With the thousand thousand Archangels and the myriad myriad of Angels, they sing unceasingly—and let all the people say with them:

Holy, holy, holy
is the Lord Sabaoth.
Heaven and earth are filled with his glory.
Blessed is he for ever. Amen.

[The Account of the Institution]

The bishop continues:

You are truly holy, most holy,
Most High, exalted for ever.
Holy too is your Only-begotten Son,
our Lord and God, Jesus Christ . . .
He was born of the Virgin,
he took flesh, he who is God and Word,
well-beloved Son, "first born of every creature."
According to the prophecies made of him,
he came of the stock of David and Abraham,
of the tribe of Judah . . .

he, the Judge, was judged,
given over to the governor Pilate,
he was condemned, he the savior.
He was fixed to the cross
though he ought not to have known suffering,
He died,
though he is immortal by nature.
He was buried,
though it is he who gives life,
to deliver his own from suffering,
to rescue them from death,
to break the fetters of the devil
and free men from his deceit.
He rose from the dead on the third day,
dwelt among his disciples for forty days,
ascended into heaven
and sits at your right hand, his God and Father.
We then, recalling the sufferings which he endured for us,
give you thanks, almighty God,
not as well as we ought,
but as well as we can,
and fulfill his last testament.

For on the night when he was betrayed,
he took bread in his holy and spotless hands,
and, lifting his eyes to heaven
towards you, God and Father,
he broke it and gave it to his disciples, saying:
"This is the mystery of the New Covenant.
Take and eat of it:
This is my body which is broken for many
for the forgiveness of sins. . . .

He also filled the cup with wine mixed with water,
blessed it and gave it to them, saying:
"Drink of this, all of you, this is my blood,
which is poured out for many for the forgiveness of sins.
Do this in memory of me.
For each time that you eat this bread

and that you drink this cup
you proclaim my death
until I come."

[Anamnesis]

Mindful then of his passion and death,
of his resurrection from among the dead,
of his return to heaven,
and of his second coming
when he will come with glory and power
to judge the living and the dead
and render to each according to his works,
we offer you, O King and God,
according to his commandment, this bread and this cup.
We thank you through him
for having judged us worthy to stand before you
and exercise this priesthood for you.
And we beg you
to look down graciously
on these offerings which we bring you,
O God, who has need of nothing,
and to accept them as pleasing to you,
in honor of your Christ.

[Epiclesis]

Send down upon this sacrifice your Holy Spirit,
"Witness of the sufferings of the Lord Jesus,"
that he may make this bread
the Body of Christ,
and this cup
the blood of Christ.
May those who share in it
be strengthened for devotion,
obtain forgiveness of sins,
be delivered from the devil and his errors,
be filled with the Holy Spirit,
become worthy of your Christ,

enter into possession of eternal life
and be reconciled with you, almighty God.

[There follows lengthy intercessory litanies by both the bishop and deacon, very similar to the "Litany for the Faithful" which was prayed after the "Dismissal of the Catechumens."]

COMMUNION LITURGY

[Preparatory Prayer]

The bishop says:

> "Great God, whose name is sublime,
> who are magnificent in your designs
> and powerful in your works" (Jer 32. 18–19),
> God and Father of Jesus,
> your holy Son, our Savior:
> Cast your eyes upon us, upon your flock here,
> whom you have chosen through Christ,
> to the glory of your name.
> Sanctify us body and soul,
> "cleanse us from all defilement
> of flesh and spirit" (2 Cor 7,1).
> Grant us the good things here present.
> Do not judge any among us unworthy,
> but be our help, succor and defense,
> through your Christ, with whom
> glory, honor and praise,
> glorification and thanksgiving,
> to you, and to the Holy Spirit,
> for ever. Amen.

[Acclamation of the People]

When everyone has replied: Amen, the deacon says:
> Attend.

The bishop then addresses the people in these words:
> "Holy things to the holy."

The people are to reply:

> One Holy One, one Lord,
> Jesus Christ, who is blessed for ever,
> to the glory of the Father. Amen.

> "Glory to God in the highest,
> and on earth, peace,
> among men, good will [of God]."
> Hosanna to the Son of David.
> Blessed be he who comes in the name of the Lord.
> God the Lord has shown himself to us.
> "Hosanna in the highest heaven."

[The Rite of Communion]

[The bishop then communicates, followed by the priests, the deacons, the subdeacons, the readers, the singers and the monks; then, among the women, the deaconesses, the virgins and the widows; then the children; then the rest of the people, in order, with reverence and devotion, without disturbance.]

As he gives the oblation, the bishop says:
   "The Body of the Lord."

He who receives it is to reply:
   "Amen."

Let the deacon take the cup and say as he gives it:
   "The blood of Christ, the cup of life."

He who drinks is to respond:
   "Amen."

(While communion is going on, Psalm thirty-three is recited.)

When all the men and women have communicated, the deacons are to take what is left over and carry it to the sacristy.

[Prayer after Communion]

When the psalmist has finished, the deacon is to say:

Having received the precious body and blood of Christ, let us give thanks to him who has made us worthy to participate in his holy mysteries.

Let us beg him that they be not our condemnation,
but our salvation,
the well-being of soul and body,
the safeguard of devotion, the forgiveness of sins,
the life of the world to come.

Let us rise. Through the grace of Christ, let us recommend ourselves to the unbegotten God and to his Christ.

[Prayer of Thanksgiving]

The bishop is to say the prayer of thanksgiving:

Lord God almighty,
Father of your Christ, your blessed Son,
you who hear those who call on you uprightly,
who recognize even the prayers we make in silence:
We give you thanks for having judged us worthy
to participate in your holy mysteries.
You have given them to us
to strengthen in us the certainty
of the good things we already know,
for the safeguard of devotion,
for the forgiveness of sins,
for the name of Christ has been invoked upon us
and we have made our dwelling near to you.
You have separated us from the company of the unjust,
join us to those who are consecrated to you.
Strengthened in the truth by the coming of the Holy Spirit,
show us that which we do not know,
fill up our deficiencies,
confirm that which we know.
Preserve the priests blameless in your service,

keep kings in peace,
magistrates in justice.
Give us favorable weather,
harvests in abundance.
Keep the world in your almighty Providence,
pacify the nations who desire war,
convert those who are in error.
Sanctify your people,
protect the virgins,
keep the married in fidelity,
confirm those who live in chastity,
help the little children to grow,
strengthen the neophytes,
teach the catechumens,
and make them worthy of initiation.
Gather us all in the Kingdom of heaven,
in Christ Jesus our Lord,
with whom glory, honor and worship
be to you, and to the Holy Spirit,
for ever. Amen.

[Final Blessing]

Let the deacon say: Bow your heads before God, through his Christ, and receive the blessing.

The bishop then prays in this way:

Almighty God, true and without compare . . .
God of Israel, your people who truly see,
who believe in Christ:
Be gracious, hear me for the sake of your name,
and bless those who have bowed their heads
"Grant them the requests of their hearts" (Ps 37,4),
those which are for their good,
do not cast any of them out of your Kingdom.
Sanctify them, keep them, protect them, help them,
deliver them from the Adversary, from every enemy.
Watch over their dwellings,
"Keep their coming in and their going out" (Ps 121,8).

Glory to you, praise and splendor,
worship and adoration,
and to your Son, Jesus, your Christ,
our Lord, God and King,
and to the Holy Spirit,
now and always,
and for ever and ever.
Amen.

[Dismissal]

The deacon says:
    "Go in peace."

CHAPTER EIGHT

THE ANAPHORAS OF BASIL AND JOHN CHRYSOSTOM

The Liturgies of Basil the Great (d. 379) and John Chrysostom (d. 407) are two of three Liturgies regularly celebrated by Eastern Christians who trace their origin to Constantinople. The former has been influenced by the latter and both have affinities with one attributed to Saint James the Apostle. The liturgy that became most widespsread, especially among the Slavs in the Balkans and in Russia, was the liturgy of Constantinople, which is named, with only limited justification, after St. John Chrysostom. This liturgy which is of Antiochene-Cappadocian origin, gradually replaced to a great extent the Liturgy of St. Basil, which was likewise used in early Constantinople, and also influenced practice at Alexandria and in Armenia. Many western Christians think of this Liturgy of St. John Chrysostom as being the liturgy of the Eastern Church. Immigration to the western hemisphere meant that the Eastern Christians brought their liturgies with them. The Liturgies are completely sung and in their dialogical character, the use of the vernacular, and the reception of the Eucharist under the species of bread and wine, anticipated by many years the changes which took place in the Roman Liturgy only after the Second Vatican Council.

The Liturgy of St. Basil is also in use in the Eastern Church, but on only ten days in the year. The Anaphora is a highly developed version of the one attributed to Basil of Caesarea. Parallels have been found in the writing of St. Basil the Great, who is generally believed to have added the biblical citations. Antioch and Caesarea sent as bishops to Constantinople Gregory of Nazianzus, Nectarius and John Chrysostom, who brought with them the liturgy of Cappadocia composed by St. Basil. From Constantinople it spread throughout Eastern Christianity and was in use until, as noted, the considerably shorter version attributed to Chrysostom largely replaced it. At several

*points it is similar, even identical, to the Liturgy of St. John Chrysostom, which this **anaphora** probably influenced. Noteworthy in Basil's **anaphora** is its expression in what is a tapestry of scriptural texts of praise and thanksgiving for the goodness of God revealed in Christ. Because of its length the "Great Intercession" is not included below, although its proper place is indicated within the text. The shorter version which appears in **The Anaphora** of John Chrysostom provides an idea of the breadth of prayerful concern it expresses. An adequate discussion of the **epiclesis**, explicit in the East and vague in the West, and the theological problems associated with it, is not possible here. The wording of Basil, representative of Eastern Liturgies, is a petition that the Holy Spirit come upon both the gifts and the community, making the gifts the body and blood of Christ and sanctifying the community. To be noted as well is the similarity of the prayers preceding and following the Institution Narratives to the more recent Roman Eucharistic Prayers. **The Anaphora** of St. Basil delights in piling up synonyms. The following translation permits itself some compression.*
[Translation: Hamman, 70–77]

THE ANAPHORA OF ST. BASIL

[Preface]

. . . It is right and proper and a fitting tribute to your majesty that we should give you thanks and glory, O God in very truth, and with pure hearts and humble minds offer you this sacrifice of praise, for you have given us knowledge of your truth.

Who can adequately tell the extent of your power, or sound your praises, or describe your wonders? Sovereign Ruler of all that is, Lord of heaven and earth and of all other creatures, visible and invisible: you sit on your glorious throne and look down into the depths; you are eternal and invisible, O Father of our Lord Jesus Christ; and he is the Image of your goodness, the Seal that presents a faithful copy of your own nature, O Father; the living Word, truly God, eternal Wisdom, Life, Source of holiness and power. He is the true Light, and through him has been revealed the Holy Spirit, the Spirit of Truth, the grace of adoption, pledge of the inheritance that is to come and foretaste of the blessings of eternity. He is the power that gives life, the fount whence holiness flows; and in the strength that comes from him, every creature endowed with mind and spirit does you service and continually gives you glory, for all things are your servants. For the angels, archangels, thrones, dominations, principalities, virtues and powers, and the cherubim with their many eyes praise you. The six-winged seraphim stand around you too, hiding their faces with two of their wings, hiding their feet with two more, with the other two flying. They cry out to one another, never resting their voices, never sinking into silence as they proclaim your glory and say:

[Sanctus]

Holy, holy, holy is the God of hosts. Heaven and earth are full of your glory. Hosannah in the highest. Blessed is he that comes in the name of the Lord. Hosannah in the highest.

[Priest] . . . Holy you are indeed, and all holy, no limit can be set to the splendor of your holiness; wise and judicious are all your ordinances, for in righteousness and true judgment you brought all things to us.

You fashioned man from the dust of the earth, did him the honor of making him in your own image, O God, set him in a delightful garden and promised that if he did what you told him, he should live for ever and enjoy the blessings of eternity. But he disobeyed your orders, true God though you were his Creator; he was led astray by the cunning of the serpent and, becoming the victim of his own sins, he was made subject to death. By that righteous decree of yours, O God, he was driven out of paradise into this world and returned to the earth from which he had been taken.

But you provided a means of salvation for him: it would be possible for him to be born again in your Christ. You were too kind to cast off forever the creature you had made, O good one; you promoted his welfare in many different ways, so great was your mercy. You sent him the prophets; you worked miracles through the saints, who generation after generation gave you pleasure; you gave the law for our assistance; you set angels over us to guard us.

When the appointed time came, you spoke through your Son himself, through whom you had created this temporal world. He is the radiance of your splendor and the full expression of your being; he upholds all things by his powerful word: he thought it no usurpation to claim equality with God, for he was God himself from all eternity. Your Son appeared on earth and lived among men; he took flesh of Mary, the virgin; he accepted the lot of a slave and assumed the body that is the sign of man's humble condition, as a prelude to assuming us into his own glorious body.

Since through man sin came into the world and through sin death, your only Son, who was in your bosom throughout eternity, yet was born of a woman, the holy Mother of God and ever-virgin Mary, born under the law, was pleased to condemn sin in flesh of his own that they who died because of Adam were to receive life because of Christ. He lived in the world as a citizen of it and told us what to do to obtain salvation; he placed us where the errors of idolatry could not reach us and he taught us to know you, the true God and Father; so that he acquired in us a chosen people, a royal priesthood, a consecrated nation.

He cleansed us with water and sanctified us with the Holy Spirit; he gave himself to ransom us from death, whose prisoners we were—for we had been sold, because we had sinned. Through the cross he went down into hell, bent on giving fulfilment himself to every single thing. On the third day he rose again, opening the way for all flesh to follow him (for it could not be that the forerunner of life should fall a prey to corruption); he became the first-fruits of them that had fallen asleep, the first born of the dead in every way he was to have the primacy. He went up to heaven and took his seat at your Majesty's right hand, in the highest place; and he will come back and give us all the reward our conduct deserves. He left us these reminders of his saving passion which we have set before you according to his commandments.

[Account of the Institution]

As he was going, of his own accord, to that ever memorable death which brought us life, on the night when he gave us himself that the world might live, he took bread in his hands, those pure and holy hands, and showing it to you, God and Father, gave thanks, blessed, consecrated and broke it, and gave it to his holy disciples and apostles, saying:

Take it and eat it: this is my body, broken for you, to remit your sins.

In the same way, he took the chalice with the fruit of the vine; he mixed it, gave thanks, blessed and consecrated it, and gave it to his holy disciples and apostles, saying:

Drink from it, all of you; this is my blood, shed for you and for the multitudes, to remit your sins. Do this in memory of me. Every time you eat this bread and drink this cup, you will be proclaiming my death and confessing my resurrection.

[Anamnesis]

We too, then, Lord, call to mind his saving sufferings and his life-giving cross, the three days he spent in the tomb, his resurrection from the dead, his going up to heaven, where he sits at your right hand, O Father, and the second coming, an occasion of glory and fear. And of all the things that are yours we offer you these, which are yours especially.

The people: We sing your praises, bless you, thank you, O Lord, and offer you our prayers, O God.

The priest: Therefore we too, all holy Master—whom you have enabled to serve at your holy altar, not for any virtue of ours (for never in our lives have we done any good) but because your mercy and compassion are so great—we too make bold to approach your altar and offer you the sacrament of the holy body and blood of your Christ.

[Epiclesis]

We beg and beseech you, holiest of all the holy, in your kindness and benevolence send your Holy Spirit upon us and upon these gifts we have offered, to bless and sanctify them. May he make this bread the precious body of our Lord and God and Savior, Jesus Christ—

The deacon: Amen.

The priest:—and this chalice the precious blood of our Lord and God and Savior, Jesus Christ.

The deacon: Amen.

The priest:—shed that the world may have life.

The deacon: Amen.

The priest: May all of us that share the one bread and the one chalice be united with one another into fellowship in the one Holy Spirit. May the reception of the holy body and blood of your Christ bring judgment and condemnation to none of us. May we find mercy and grace with all the saints who have ever given you pleasure since the beginning of time. . . .

[Then comes the Great Intercession.]

And grant that with one voice and heart we may praise and glorify your name in the fullness of its holiness and splendor, O Father, Son and Holy Spirit, now and for ever, age after age. Amen.

THE ANAPHORA OF ST. JOHN CHRYSOSTOM

[Preface]

It is right and proper that we should hymn you and give you praise and thanks and worship wherever your power is felt, for no word can express you, O God, no mind understand you, no eye behold you, no intelligence grasp you—you who have existed from all eternity and have always been the same: you and your only Son and your Holy Spirit. You it was that drew us out of nothingness into existence, and when we fell, raised us up again; you spared no effort until you had brought us to heaven and bestowed upon us the kingdom that is to come.

We thank you for all these blessings—you and your only Son and your Holy Spirit; we thank you, too, for all the other blessings you have given us, those we are aware of and those of which we know nothing, those that we see and those that we cannot see. We thank you for this ministry, which you have consented to accept at our hands, even though the archangels throng in their thousands and angels in their tens of thousands, the cherubim also and the seraphim, each with his six wings and his many eyes, each borne aloft and flying, each one chanting, proclaiming, shouting the hymn of triumph, as they say:

[Sanctus]

The people: Holy, holy, holy is the Lord of hosts. Heaven and earth are full of your glory. Hosanna in the highest.

The priest: With these blessed powers we too cry out to you, Master, for we know how you love man. Holy you are, we say, all-holy; you and your Only-begotten Son and your Holy Spirit. Holy you are, and all-holy, splendid indeed is your glory. Such was your love for the world that you gave up your Only-begotten Son; no one who believed in him was to perish: they were all to have eternal life.

[Institution Narrative]

So, then, he came; and when he had done all that he was meant to do for us, on the night when he was given up—or rather, when he gave himself up, he took bread in his holy and undefiled and blameless hands, gave thanks, blessed it, broke it, and gave it to his holy disciples and apostles, saying:

Take it and eat it: this is my body, broken for you, to remit your sins.

When the supper was over, he did the same with the chalice, saying: Drink from it, all of you: this is my blood, the blood of the new covenant, shed for you and for the multitudes, to remit your sins.

[Anamnesis]

Calling, then, to mind, the holy commandment and all that has been done for us; remembering the cross, the burial, the resurrection on the third day, the going up to heaven, where he sits at the right hand, and the second coming again in his glory: of the things that are yours we offer you these, in all and through all.

The people: We sing your praises, bless you and thank you and offer you our prayers, O God.

[Epiclesis]

The priest: We offer you, too, this spiritual sacrifice, which requires no shedding of blood. We beg and beseech you, we implore you, send down your Holy Spirit upon us and upon these gifts we have offered; make this bread the precious body of your Christ (changing it by your Holy Spirit) and make what is in this chalice your Christ's precious blood (changing it by your Holy Spirit). To those who receive them may these gifts bring temperance of soul, forgiveness of sins, the fellowship of the Holy Spirit, full possession of the kingdom of heaven and a confident approach to you; may they not lead to judgment and condemnation.

We offer you this spiritual sacrifice for those of our ancestors and fathers who had the faith and are now at rest; in memory of the patriarchs, prophets, apostles, preachers, evangelists, martyrs and confessors and those who lived continently; and for the spirits of all the just who grew perfect in the faith.

Especially do we offer it for our lady Mary, the all holy, unspotted, more than blessed, glorious, mother of God and ever virgin.

[At this point the diptychs containing the names of the dead are read.]

We offer the sacrifice for Saint John, the prophet, precursor and baptist; of the holy apostles, glorious and illustrious; of Saint N., whose feast we are celebrating; and of all your other saints. May their prayers prevail upon you to regard us with favor. Remember too, all who have fallen asleep confident of rising again and living for all eternity; give them rest where the light shines from your face.

Again we pray you, remember, Lord, all the orthodox bishops who faithfully teach your word, the true word, remember all their priests, the deacons serving Christ, and every other degree of the hierarchy.

Again, we offer you this spiritual sacrifice for the whole world, for the holy, Catholic, and apostolic Church, for those whose lives are dignified by chastity, for our eminently faithful and Christ loving kings, and for all their household and army. Grant them a peaceful reign, O Lord, that sharing in their tranquillity we too may live calm and tranquil lives with devotion and dignity.

[Here the diptychs with the names of the living are read.]

Remember, Lord, the city where we live, and every other city and district; remember those dwelling in them in the faith.

Remember, Lord, those who are traveling, whether by land or by sea; remember the sick, the suffering and those who are held in captivity; remember to grant them all salvation.

Remember, Lord, all who are bearing fruit and doing good works in your holy churches and seeing to the needs of the poor; and send down your mercy on us all.

And grant that with one voice and heart we may praise and glorify your name in the fullness of its holiness and splendor, O Father, Son and Holy Spirit, now and for ever, age after age. Amen.

CHAPTER NINE

THE ROMAN CANON

*The Eucharistic Prayer given here, with the exception of some later additions, is over fifteen hundred years old. For four hundred years, until the year 1968 and the introduction of the Missal of Paul VI, it was the only Eucharistic Prayer with which Roman Catholics were familiar. It had taken shape by the second half of the fourth century, possibly in the time of Pope Damasus I, who gave to the liturgy its specifically Latin cast. Known as the "Canon" (a Greek word which means the measuring rod which builders used), the term as used to describe the center piece of the Mass, is a short expression for "Canon gratiarum actio," which means "the norm to be followed in giving thanks." As has been noted many times, the Canon has affinities with the Eucharistic Prayer of Hippolytus, with a significant difference in style. Whereas that of Hippolytus proceeds by a series of relative clauses in an unbroken flow to the final doxology, the Roman Canon consists of more or less independent pieces of prose strung together with the institution narrative as its center. In place of the earlier freedom granted to the celebrant in antiquity and attested to by **The Didache**, Justin, and even the arch conservative, Hippolytus, the Roman Canon allows of almost no variations, except for the preface which varied according to the season or the nature of the celebration, and some minor seasonal insertions in the prayers known as the "Communicantes" and "Quam oblationem." Structurally solid, it strikes many contemporaries as somewhat cold by comparison with either earlier Western liturgies or present Eastern liturgies such as that attributed to Chrysostom. There are no Roman witnesses for the Latin Canon in its earlier stages. St. Ambrose of Milan in his **De Sacramentis** (IV, 5, 21–26, 27) preserved a form of some key passages of it. It appears that this Roman Eucharistic Prayer was quickly taken as a model in other Latin-speaking areas.*

The various intercessory prayers (with lists of saints) are not mentioned by Ambrose but are mentioned by Popes Innocent I

(401–417), Boniface I (418–422), and Celestine I (422–432). Thus, the Canon must have acquired its present form soon after the year 400. Once said aloud in a voice clearly audible to the community grouped around him, in time, with the shift in emphasis to awe and mystery, the priest prayed the Canon in a voice which could be heard only by those very close to the altar within the sanctuary. It is significant that in the Roman Missal in use until 1971, the title introducing the Canon read "infra actionem," that is, within the act of thanksgiving. In continuity with the best in tradition, the prayer is part of an act which from beginning to end is an act of thanksgiving and praise. The insertion of the Sanctus, probably in the fifth century, after the one most often varied prayer, the Preface, had the unfortunate effect of limiting the understanding of what constituted the Eucharistic Prayer to what followed the Sanctus. Because this hymn was often sung in a prolonged manner either by choir or congregation, while in the meantime the celebrant continued to pray the Canon in silence, the Canon became the prayer of the celebrant alone rather than of the entire worshiping community.

Of all parts of the Roman Canon it is the Preface which retains the character of the early Eucharist (in its structure of dialogue, praise, and acclamation) and reveals its heritage in the Jewish berakah, prayers of blessing and thanksgiving. The complex structure of the Canon made it difficult for the praying community to understand it fully. It refers to frequently unknown saints, the epiclesis is much too vague, and the eschatological element, intrinsic to the Last Supper itself as well as the tradition, is lacking. In the light of contemporary historical and liturgical studies its shortcomings have become clear. Nevertheless it merits great respect not only because of its antiquity and the witness it bears to eucharistic doctrine but also because it nourished the faith and devotion of countless Christians for centuries.
[Translation: Vagaggini, pp. 331–334.]

THE ROMAN CANON

I

The Lord be with you.
And with you.
Let us lift up our hearts.

We have raised them up to the Lord.
Let us give thanks to the Lord our God.
It is right and fitting.

II

It is right and fitting, good and just, that we should always give thanks to you for all things. Lord, holy Father, almighty eternal God, who in your incomparable goodness were pleased to make light shine in darkness when you sent Jesus Christ to us as protector of our souls. For our salvation he humbled himself, and subjected himself to death, so as to restore to us that immortality which Adam had lost, and to make us God's heirs and sons.

III

For such goodness and generosity we can never praise and thank you sufficiently, and so we ask you in your great love and compassion kindly to accept this sacrifice which we offer you in the presence of your divine goodness, through Jesus Christ our Lord and God.

IV

Through him we humbly ask and pray you, almighty Father, to accept and bless these gifts, these pure offerings. We offer them to you, first of all, for your holy Catholic Church: be pleased to give peace to her, spread over all the earth (We offer them to you at the same time, for our blessed bishop, N., and for all the bishops faithful to the true doctrine, who are the guardians of the apostolic faith).

Remember also, Lord, your servants who address their prayers to you, the living and true God, in honor of your saints, N. N., for the forgiveness of their sins.

V

(Send, Lord, your Holy Spirit from heaven) and mercifully bless and accept this offering which is the image and likeness of the body and blood of Jesus Christ your Son, our redeemer.

VI

For on the day before he suffered, he took bread into his holy and blessed hands, looked up to heaven, to you, holy Father, almighty eternal God, and giving thanks, blessed and broke it and gave it to his apostles and disciples, saying: "Take and eat this, all of you, for this is my body, that will be broken for you." In the same way, on the day before he suffered, after he had eaten, he took the cup into his holy and blessed hands, looked up to heaven, to you, holy Father, almighty eternal God, and giving thanks, blessed and gave it to his apostles and disciples, saying: "Take and drink of this, all of you, for this is my blood which shall be poured out for you and for everyone to take away all sins. Each time that you do this, you will do it in memory of me until I return."

VII

That is why, mindful of his most glorious passion and of his resurrection from the dead and ascension into heaven, we offer you this spotless victim, this unbloody victim, this holy bread and cup of eternal life.

VIII

And we ask and pray you to accept this offering carried by your angels to your heavenly altar, as you wished also to accept the gifts of your just servant Abel, the sacrifice of Abraham, father of our race, and the offering of your high priest Melchisidech.

IX

(We ask you that through the grace of the Holy Spirit the gift of your love may be confirmed in us, and that we may possess in eternal glory what we already receive from your goodness.)

X

Through our Lord, Jesus Christ, in whom and with whom honor, praise, glory, might and power are yours with the Holy Spirit, from the beginning, now and always, for ever and ever. Amen.

CHAPTER TEN

THE RITE OF CHRISTIAN INITIATION

*The publication in 1972 of the complex of rites, the **Christian Initiation of Adults**, now popularly known as the RCIA, represented the result of efforts begun in 1962. In that year, Pope John XXIII authorized a ritual of baptism in stages. This was a first response to the requests of the Church in France and the third world for a rite of initiation which would meet the needs of the Church in the modern world. Revised in 1968 and in 1974, the present **Rite of Christian Initiation of Adults** was made mandatory in the Dioceses of the United States in 1988. Most noteworthy is the restoration of the catechumenate, of sufficient length and seriousness to ensure its purpose, which had been one of the major demands of the Second Vatican Council.*

The process of initiation consists of four periods of development and three stages of threshold events, which are marked by various "rites of initiation."

The first step on the way of conversion is the "Precatechumenate," a period of inquiry on the part of an interested person and of explanation or evangelization on the part of the local community. Its purpose is to allow the desire of following Christ within the Church to mature.

The dispositions manifested during this stage of inquiry are ritualized by the rite of becoming a catechumen. At this point the inquirers manifest their serious intention of entering the Church, and the Church with corresponding seriousness admits them to the Catechumenate by writing their names in the "Register of Catechumens." From this point on, the catechumens are joined to the Church and one who marries another catechumen or an unbaptized person during this time is married with the appropriate Church ritual. A catechumen who dies during this period receives Christian burial. The catechumenate is an extended period during which the candidates are given pastoral formation and trained by suitable discipline.

Through instruction, participation in liturgies of the word and prayer services, and active participation in the Church's mission to spread the Gospel, the catechumen gradually assumes a new outlook and moral stance with the social consequences such a change brings with it. The length of the catechumenate cannot be determined beforehand. Its duration depends upon the progress of the catechumen in the Church's way of life.

The period of the catechumenate culminates with the community's election of the catechumens for the reception of the sacraments of initiation, at the next celebration of the sacraments of initiation, ideally if not always, at the conclusion of Lent, during the Holy Saturday Vigil of Easter. The election with its concomitant rite of enrollment in the book of the elect, is a solemn moment, a turning point in the whole process of the catechumenate. During this period of even more intense preparation, various rites, especially the scrutinies and presentations, are celebrated. The purposes of these rites is to free the elect from sin and to strengthen them in Christ. The presentations of the Creed and the Lord's Prayer leads them to further enlightenment and illumination.

The next and most important stage is the reception of the sacraments of baptism, confirmation, and the Eucharist in a single celebration. The elect are now fully incorporated into the ecclesial body of the people of God.

The Church's care for its new members does not end with the rites of initiation. In the weeks that follow, the neophytes' instruction and incorporation continue in the period of postbaptismal catechesis or "mystagogia."

*Any description of the extraordinarily rich process of initiation must emphasize the fact that initiation is a **process** through which a person responding to the grace of Christ, and helped at every step by the whole community, turns with complete seriousness and maturity of purpose from previous attitudes, dispositions, and values to those which should characterize a member of the Body of Christ. Not only is the catechumen assisted by the community but he or she by the seriousness of witness with which they approach initiation provides the community with the opportunity to respond ever more generously to the God who continues to summon it to continuing conversion of mind and heart.*

The rite of the conferral of the sacraments of Baptism, Confirmation, and Eucharist is given here. Elements which have been noted in the rites from the time of antiquity will be readily noted in the contemporary rite; the blessing of the baptismal water, the renunciation, anointing, profession of faith, the threefold immersion or infusion, the laying on of hands and the sealing with chrism. As in the early Church, baptism and confirmation are followed by the Eucharist. The rites of antiquity have not simply been recovered, they have been given new life to meet a new generation of those becoming Christians. In the translation of the celebration of the rites of initiation given here, the explanatory notes which precede the rite, (nn. 198–211) constituting as they do a contemporary counterpart to the patristic commentaries on the rites, have been retained.

[Translation: Excerpts from the English translation of *Rite of Christian Initiation of Adults* © 1988, International Committee on English in the Liturgy, Inc., All Rights Reserved.]

THIRD STEP: CELEBRATION OF THE SACRAMENTS OF INITIATION

*When we were baptized we joined Jesus in death
so that we might walk in the newness of his life*

198. The third step in the Christian initiation of adults is the celebration of the sacraments of baptism, confirmation, and Eucharist. Through this final step the elect, receiving pardon for their sins, are admitted into the people of God. They are graced with adoption as children of God and are led by the Holy Spirit into the promised fullness of time begun in Christ (*Lumen Gentium*, no. 48, also Ephesians 1.10), and as they share in the Eucharistic sacrifice and meal, even to a foretaste of the kingdom of God.

199. The usual time for the celebration of the sacraments of initiation is the Easter Vigil, at which preferably the bishop himself presides as celebrant, at least for the initiation of those who are fourteen years old or older. As indicated in the Roman Missal, "Easter Vigil," no. 44, the conferral of the sacraments follows the blessing of the water.

200. When the celebration takes place outside the usual time, care should be taken to ensure that it has a markedly paschal character.
. . .

CELEBRATION OF BAPTISM

201. The celebration of baptism has as its center and high point the baptismal washing and the invocation of the Holy Trinity. Beforehand there are rites that have an inherent relationship to the baptismal washing: first, the blessing of water, then the renunciation of sin by the elect, their anointing with the oil of catechumens, and their profession of faith. Following the baptismal washing, the effects received through this sacrament are given expression in the explanatory rites: the anointing with chrism (when confirmation does not immediately follow baptism), the clothing with a white garment, and the presentation of a lighted candle.

202.   PRAYER OVER THE WATER: The celebration of baptism begins with the blessing of water. . . . The blessing declares the religious meaning of water as God's creation and the sacramental use of water in the unfolding of the paschal mystery, and the blessing is also a remembrance of God's wonderful works in the history of salvation.

The blessing thus introduces an invocation of the Trinity at the very outset of the celebration of baptism. For it calls to mind the mystery of God's love from the beginning of the world and the creation of the human race; by invoking the Holy Spirit and proclaiming Christ's death and resurrection, it impresses on the mind the newness of Christian baptism, by which we share in his own death and resurrection and receive the holiness of God himself.

203. RENUNCIATION OF SIN AND PROFESSION OF FAITH: In their renunciation of sin and profession of faith those to be baptized express their explicit faith in the paschal mystery that has already been recalled in the blessing of water and that will be connoted by the words of the sacrament soon to be spoken by the baptizing minister. Adults are not saved unless they come forward of their own accord and with the will to accept God's gift through their own belief. The faith of those to be baptized is not simply the faith of the Church, but the personal faith of each one of them and each one of them is expected to keep it a living faith.

Therefore the renunciation of sin and the profession of faith are an apt prelude to baptism, the sacrament of that faith by which the elect hold fast to God and receive new birth from him. Because of the renunciation of sin and the profession of faith, which form the one rite, the elect will not be baptized merely passively but will receive this great sacrament with the active resolve to renounce error and to hold fast to God. By their own personal act in the rite of renouncing sin and professing their faith, the elect, as was prefigured in the first covenant with the patriarchs, renounce sin and Satan in order to commit themselves for ever to the promise of the Savior and to the mystery of the Trinity. By professing their faith before the celebrant and the entire community, the elect express the intention, developed to maturity during the preceding periods of initiation, to enter into a new covenant with Christ. Thus these adults embrace the faith that through divine help the Church has handed down, and are baptized in that faith.

204. ANOINTING WITH THE OIL OF CATECHUMENS: The anointing with the oil of catechumens takes place between the renunciation and the profession of faith, unless this anointing has been anticipated in the preparation rites of Holy Saturday or the conference of bishops has decreed its omission from the baptismal rites. This anointing symbolized the need of the elect for God's help and strength so that, undeterred by the bonds of the past and overcoming the opposition of the devil, they will forthrightly take the step of professing their faith and will hold fast to it unfalteringly throughout their lives.

205. BAPTISM: Immediately after their profession of living faith in Christ's paschal mystery, the elect come forward and receive that mystery as expressed in the washing with water; thus once the elect have professed faith in the Father, Son and Holy Spirit, invoked by the celebrant, the divine persons act so that those they have chosen receive adoption and become members of the people of God.

206. Therefore in the celebration of baptism the washing with water should take on its full importance as the sign of that mystical sharing in Christ's death and resurrection through which those who believe in his name die to sin and rise to eternal life. Either immersion or the pouring of water should be chosen for the rite, whichever will serve in individual cases and in the various traditions and circumstances to ensure the clear understanding that this washing is not a mere purification rite but the sacrament of being joined to Christ.

207. EXPLANATORY RITES: The baptismal washing is followed by rites that give expression to the effects of the sacrament just received. The anointing with chrism is a sign of the royal priesthood of the baptized and that they are now numbered in the company of the people of God. The clothing with the white garment signifies the new dignity they have received. The presentation of a lighted candle shows that they are called to walk as befits the children of the light.

CELEBRATION OF CONFIRMATION

208. In accord with the ancient practice followed in the Roman liturgy, adults are not to be baptized without receiving confirmation immediately afterward, unless some serious reason stands in the way. The conjunction of the two celebrations signifies the unity of the paschal mystery, the close link between the mission of the Son and the outpouring of the Holy Spirit, and the connection between the two sacraments through which the Son and the Holy Spirit come with the Father to those who are baptized.

209. Accordingly, confirmation is conferred after the explanatory rites of baptism, the anointing after baptism being omitted.

THE NEOPHYTES' FIRST SHARING IN THE CELEBRATION OF THE EUCHARIST

210. Finally in the celebration of the Eucharist, as they take part for the first time and with full right, the newly baptized reach the culminating point in their Christian initiation. In this Eucharist the neophytes, now raised to the ranks of the royal priesthood, have an active part in both the general intercessions and, to the extent possible, in bringing the gifts to the altar. With the entire community they share in the offering of the sacrifice and say the Lord's Prayer, giving expression to the spirit of adoption as God's children that they have received in baptism. When in communion they receive the body that was given for us and the blood that was shed, the neophytes are strengthened in the gifts they have already received and are given a foretaste of the eternal banquet.

CELEBRATION OF THE SACRAMENTS OF INITIATION

(Easter Vigil)

CELEBRATION OF BAPTISM

211. The celebration of baptism begins after the homily. It takes place at the baptismal font, if this is in view of the faithful; otherwise in the sanctuary, where a vessel of water for the rite should be prepared beforehand.

INVITATION TO PRAYER

213. The celebrant addresses the following or a similar invitation for the assembly to join in prayer for the candidates.

Dear Friends: Let us pray to Almighty God for our brothers and sisters, N. and N., who are asking for baptism. He has called them and brought them to this moment. May he grant them light and strength to follow Christ with resolute hearts and to profess the faith of the Church. May he give them the new life of the Holy Spirit, the Spirit whom we are about to ask to come down upon this water.

[Litany]

PRAYER OVER THE WATER

215. After the Litany of the Saints, the celebrant blesses the water.
Father,
you give us grace through sacramental signs
which tell us of the wonders of your unseen power.

In baptism we use your gift of water,
which you have made a rich symbol of the grace
you give us in this sacrament.

At the very dawn of creation
your Spirit breathed on the waters,
making them the wellspring of all holiness.

The waters of the great flood
you made a sign of the waters of baptism
that make an end of sin
and a new beginning of goodness.

Through the waters of the Red Sea
you led Israel out of slavery
to be an image of God's holy people
set free from sin by baptism.

In the waters of the Jordan
your Son was baptized by John
and anointed with the Spirit.

Your Son willed that water and blood should flow
from his side as he hung upon the cross.

After his resurrection he told his disciples:
"Go out and teach all nations,
baptizing them in the name of the Father,
and of the Son, and of the Holy Spirit."

Father,
look now with love upon your Church
and unseal for it the fountain of baptism.

By the power of the Holy Spirit
give to this water the grace of your Son.
so that in the sacrament of baptism
all those whom you have created in your likeness
may be cleansed from sin
and rise to a new birth of innocence
by water and the Spirit.

Here, if this can be done conveniently, the celebrant before continuing lowers the Easter candle into the water once or three times, then holds it there until the acclamation at the end of the blessing.

We ask you, Father, with your Son
to send the Holy Spirit upon the water of this font.
May all who are buried with Christ in the death of baptism
rise also with him to newness of life.
We ask this through Christ our Lord.

All: Amen.

The people say the following or some other suitable acclamation.

Springs of water, bless the Lord.
Give him glory and praise for ever.

RENUNCIATION OF SIN

Celebrant:
    Do you reject sin so as to live in the freedom of God's children?

Candidates:
    I do.

Celebrant:
    Do you reject the glamour of evil and refuse to be mastered by sin?

Candidates:
    I do.

Celebrant:
    Do you reject Satan, father of sin and prince of darkness?

Candidates:
    I do:

(Two other optional formularies are given)

219. Then the celebrant, informed again of each candidate's name by the godparents, questions the candidates individually. Each candidate is baptized immediately after his or her profession of faith.

Celebrant:

N., do you believe in God, the Father Almighty,
Creator of heaven and earth?

Candidates:

I do.

Celebrant:

Do you believe in Jesus Christ, his only Son, our Lord,
who was born of the Virgin Mary,
was crucified, died, and was buried,
rose from the dead,
and is now seated at the right hand of the Father?

Candidate:

I do.

Celebrant:

Do you believe in the Holy Spirit,
the holy Catholic Church, the communion of saints,
the forgiveness of sins, the resurrection of the body,
and the life everlasting?

Candidate:

I do.

BAPTISM

220. The celebrant baptizes each candidate either by immersion, or by the pouring of water. Each baptism may be followed by a short acclamation sung or said by the people.

If baptism is by immersion, of the whole body or of the head only, decency and decorum should be preserved. Either or both godparents touch the candidate. The celebrant, immersing the candidate's whole body or head three times, baptizes the candidate in the name of the Trinity.

N., I baptize you in the name of the Father,

[he immerses the candidate the first time]

and of the Son,

[he immerses the candidate the second time]

and of the Holy Spirit.

[he immerses the candidate the third time]

EXPLANATORY RITES

221. The celebration of baptism continues with the explanatory rites, after which the celebration of confirmation normally follows.

ANOINTING AFTER BAPTISM

222. If the confirmation of those baptized is separated from their baptism, the celebrant anoints them with chrism immediately after baptism.

[When a great number have been baptized, assisting priests or deacons may help with the anointing.]

The celebrant first says the following over all the newly baptized before the anointing.

The God of power and Father of our Lord Jesus Christ,
has freed you from sin,
and brought you to new life
through water and the Holy Spirit.

He now anoints you with the chrism of salvation,
so that, united with his people,
you may remain for ever a member of Christ
who is Priest, Prophet, and King.

Newly baptized:
Amen.

In silence each of the newly baptized is anointed with chrism on the top of the head.

CLOTHING WITH A BAPTISMAL GARMENT

223. The garment used in this rite may be white or of a color that conforms to local custom. If circumstances suggest, this rite may be omitted.

The celebrant says the following formulary, and at the words "Receive this baptismal garment" the godparents place the garment on the newly baptized.

> N. and N., you have become a new creation
> and have clothed yourselves in Christ.
> Receive this baptismal garment
> and bring it unstained to the judgment seat
> of our Lord Jesus Christ
> so that you may have everlasting life.

Newly baptized:
Amen.

PRESENTATION OF A LIGHTED CANDLE

224. The celebrant takes the Easter candle in his hands or touches it, saying to the godparents:

Godparents, please come forward to give the newly baptized the light of Christ.

A godparent of each of the newly baptized goes to the celebrant and lights a candle from the Easter candle, then presents it to the newly baptized.

Then the celebrant says to the newly baptized:

> You have been enlightened by Christ.
> Walk always as children of the light
> and keep the flame of faith alive in your hearts.
> When the Lord comes, may you go out to meet him
> with all the saints in the heavenly kingdom.

Newly baptized:
Amen.

CELEBRATION OF CONFIRMATION

INVITATION

227. The celebrant first speaks briefly to the newly baptized in these or similar words.

My dear newly baptized, born again in Christ by baptism, you have become members of Christ and of his priestly people. Now you are to share in the outpouring of the Holy Spirit among us, the Spirit sent by the Lord upon his apostles at Pentecost and given by them and their successors to the baptized.

The promised strength of the Holy Spirit, which you are to receive, will make you more like Christ and help you to be witnesses to his suffering, death, and resurrection. It will strengthen you to be active members of the Church and to build up the Body of Christ in faith and love.

With hands joined, the celebrant next addresses the people:

My dear friends, let us pray to God our Father, that he will pour out the Holy Spirit on these newly baptized to strengthen them with his gifts and anoint them to be more like Christ, the Son of God.

All pray briefly in silence.

LAYING ON OF HANDS

228. The celebrant holds his hands outstretched over the entire group of those to be confirmed and says the following prayer.

All powerful God, Father of our Lord Jesus Christ,
by water and the Holy Spirit
you freed your sons and daughters from sin
and gave them new life.

Send your Holy Spirit upon them
to be their helper and guide.

Give them the spirit of wisdom and understanding,
the spirit of right judgment and courage,

the spirit of knowledge and reverence.
Fill them will the spirit of wonder
and awe in your presence.

We ask this through Christ our Lord.

R. Amen.

ANOINTING WITH CHRISM

The minister of the sacrament dips his right thumb in the chrism and makes the sign of the cross on the forehead of the one to be confirmed as he says:

N., be sealed with the gift of the Holy Spirit.

Newly confirmed:
Amen.

The minister of the sacrament adds:
Peace be with you.

Newly confirmed:
And also with you.

230. The renewal of baptismal promises by the congregation follows the celebration of confirmation. Then the neophytes are led to their places among the faithful.

LITURGY OF THE EUCHARIST

231. Since the profession of faith is not said, the general intercessions begin immediately and for the first time the neophytes take part in them. Some of the neophytes also take part in the procession to the altar with the gifts.

233. It is most desirable that the neophytes, together with their godparents, parents, spouses, and catechists, receive communion under both kinds.

Before saying "This is the Lamb of God," the celebrant may briefly remind the neophytes of the preeminence of the Eucharist, which is the climax of their initiation and the center of the whole Christian life.

CHAPTER ELEVEN

THE MYSTAGOGICAL CATECHESIS OF ST. CYRIL OF JERUSALEM

Although the place and date of Cyril's birth are unknown, it is generally presumed that he was born in Jerusalem in 315. Made bishop of Jerusalem c. 348, suspicion arose early that he had obtained his appointment by concessions to Arianism. Actually, Cyril was in conflict with the Arians or their sympathizers from the early days of his episcopacy because of his defense of the faith proclaimed at the Council of Nicea (325) and on three occasions he was expelled from his office. He took part in the Second Council of Constantinople (381) and died a few years later, probably in 387. There is general agreement that the **Catechetical Lectures,** *instructions on the Jerusalem Creed given to the catechumens during the Lenten season about 350, are the work of Cyril as taken down in shorthand by one of his listeners. Scholars are undecided about the genuinity of the* **Mystagogical Lectures** *because of considerable differences of both style and quality in the two sets of lectures. Some ascribe them to Cyril, others to his episcopal successor in Jerusalem, John. The available evidence is inadequate to prove or disprove Cyril's authorship or to determine the precise year for the latter set of lectures. If Cyril is indeed the author, he must have delivered them toward the end of his episcopate. The irenic spirit noted in Justin is lacking in Cyril and his persistent polemic against the Jews is offensive. His exegesis of the Old Testament is implausible and unlikely to attract the modern reader.*

The principal reason for the interest the **Mystagogical Lectures** *have provoked in recent years is the wealth of detail concerning Christian initiation preserved in them and for the explanation of the symbolism of major features of initiation. Lectures 1 and 2 treat of baptism, Lecture 3 of anointing, Lectures 4 and 5 of the Eucharistic Liturgy. Worth noting in Lecture 1 is the rite of renunciation of Satan, which anyone familiar with the contemporary liturgy of the Easter Vigil will recognize as part of the "Renewal of Baptismal Promises" in the contemporary Rite of Christian Initiation of Adults. Lecture 2* *presents the rite of the profession of faith in the Trinity, followed by the stripping of clothing, symbolizing conversion from one's former way of life, and a triple immersion in the baptismal waters, symbolizing Christ's three-day burial and the baptizand's simultaneous death and rebirth, through the remission of sins and the gift of the Holy Spirit. The latter gift is emphasized by the anointing with chrism which Cyril discusses in Lecture 3. No mention is made of the conferral of the Spirit through the imposition of hands. Lecture 4 presents Cyril's teaching on the Real Presence of Christ in the symbols of bread and wine. The Eucharistic Liturgy is described from the washing of hands after the offering of the gifts of bread and wine to the communion. It will be noted that a considerable gap occurs between the description of the "Sanctus" and the epiclesis (invocation of the Holy Spirit) which effects the change of elements. A probable explanation is that Cyril is describing those rites of the liturgy which the community could see and hear, as distinguished from those parts which the celebrant said in a low voice and possibly behind a screen. The once simple Eucharist celebrated in believers' homes has, by Cyril's time, become a far more elaborate ceremony of "such high mysteries" (V,22). Cyril, as Chrysostom later, advises listeners to touch and thus to sanctify the senses with the consecrated bread and wine.*

Cyril's successor, John, a recognized disciple of Origen, is remembered primarily because he aroused the wrath of St. Jerome for offering refuge to Rufinus, an Origenist, and Pelagius, whose views on nature and grace were opposed by St. Augustine and subsequently condemned. The evidence for John's authorship is not conclusive, primarily for the lack of evidence of any significant influence of Origen in the Lectures.

[Translation: FC, 64, pp. 153–203]

FIRST LECTURE ON THE MYSTERIES

The First Part of the Baptismal Ceremony
(The Rites of the Outer Chamber:
Renunciation of Satan, Profession of Faith)
With a Lesson from Peter's First Catholic Epistle

Beginning, "Be sober, be watchful," to the End
By the same Cyril and Bishop John

1. It has long been my wish, true born and long desired children of the Church, to discourse to you upon these spiritual, heavenly mysteries. On the principle, however, that seeing is believing, I delayed until the present occasion, calculating that after what you saw on that night I should find you a readier audience now when I am to be your guide to the brighter and more fragrant meadows of this second Eden. In particular, you are now capable of understanding the diviner mysteries of divine, life-giving baptism. The time being now come to spread for you the board of more perfect instruction, let me explain the significance of what was done for you on that evening of your Baptism.

2. First you entered the antechamber of the baptistery and faced toward the west. On the command to stretch out your hand, you renounced Satan as though he were there in person. This movement, you should know, is prefigured in ancient history. When that tyrannous and cruel despot, Pharaoh, was oppressing the noble, free-spirited Hebrew nation, God sent Moses to deliver them from the hard slavery imposed upon them by the Egyptians. The doorposts were anointed with the blood of a lamb that the destroyer might pass over the houses signed with the blood; so the Jews were miraculously liberated. After their liberation the enemy gave chase, and, on seeing the sea part miraculously before them, still continued in hot pursuit, only to be instantaneously overwhelmed and engulfed in the Red Sea.

3. Pass, pray, from the old to the new, from the figure to the reality. There Moses sent by God to Egypt; here Christ sent from the Father into the world. Moses' mission was to lead out from Egypt a persecuted people; Christ's, to rescue all the people of the world who were under the tyranny of sin. There the blood of a lamb was the charm against the destroyer; here, the blood of the unspotted Lamb, Jesus Christ, is appointed your inviolable sanctuary against demons. Pharaoh pursued that people of old right into the sea; this outrageous spirit, the impudent author of all evil, followed you, each one, up to the very verge of the saving streams.

That other tyrant is engulfed and drowned in the Red Sea; this one is destroyed in the saving water.

4. You are told, however, to address him as personally present, and with arm outstretched to say: "I renounce you, Satan." Allow me to explain the reason of your facing west, for you should know it. Because the West is the region of visible darkness, Satan, who is himself darkness, has his empire in darkness—that is the significance of your looking steadily toward the west while you renounce that gloomy Prince of night.

What was it that each of you said, standing there? "I renounce you, Satan, you wicked and cruel tyrant; I no longer (you said in effect) fear your power. For Christ broke that power by sharing flesh and blood with me, planning through their assumption to break, by His death, the power of Death, to save me from subjection to perpetual bondage. I renounce you, crafty scoundrel of a serpent; I renounce you, traitor, perpetrator of every crime, who inspired our first parents to revolt. I renounce you, Satan, agent and abettor of all wickedness."

5. Then in a second phrase you are taught to say, "and all your works." All sin is "the works of Satan"; and sin, too, you must renounce, since he who has escaped from a tyrant has also cast off the tyrant's livery. Sin in all its forms, then, is included in the works of the Devil. Only let me tell you this, all your words, particularly those spoken at that awful hour, are recorded in the book of God. Whenever, therefore, you are caught in conduct contrary to your profession, you will be tried as a renegade. Renounce, then, the works of Satan, that is, every irrational deed and thought.

6. Next you say, "and all his pomp." The pomp of the devil is the craze for the theater, the horse races in the circus, the wild beast hunts, and all such vanity, from which the saint prays to God to be delivered in the words, "Turn away my eyes that they may not behold vanity" (Ps 119.37). Avoid addiction to the theater, with its spectacle of the licentiousness, the lewd and unseemly antics of actors and the frantic dancing of degenerates. Not for you, either, the folly of those who, to gratify their miserable appetite, expose themselves to wild beasts in the combats in the amphitheater. They pamper their belly at the cost of becoming themselves, in the event, food for the maw of savage beasts; of these gladiators it is fair to say that in the service of the belly which is their God they court death in the arena. Shun also the bedlam of the races, a spectacle in which souls as well as riders come to grief. All their follies are the pomp of the Devil.

7. The food, also, which is sometimes hung up in pagan temples and at festivals—meat, bread, and so forth—since it is defiled by the invocation of abominable demons, may be included in "the pomp of the Devil." For as the bread and wine of the Eucharist before the holy invocation of the adorable Trinity were ordinary bread and wine, while after the invocation the bread becomes the Body of Christ, and the wine his Blood, so these foods of the pomp of Satan, though of their own nature ordinary food, become profane through the invocation of evil spirits.

8. After this you say, "and all your service." The service of the Devil is prayer in the temples of idols, the honoring of lifeless images, the lighting of lamps or the burning of incense by springs or streams; there have been cases of persons who, deceived by dreams or by evil spirits, have gone to this length in the hope of being rewarded by the cure of even bodily ailments. Have nothing to do with these practices. The observation of birds, divination, omens, charms and amulets, magic and similar chicanery—all such practices are the cult of the Devil. Shun them. For if you should succumb to such practices after renouncing Satan and transferring your allegiance to Christ, you will find the usurper more cruel than ever. For if formerly, treating you as a familiar, he abated the rigors of your slavery, now he will be furiously exasperated against you. So you will lose Christ and taste Satan's tyranny. Have you not heard the old story which recounts the fate of Lot and his daughters. Was not Lot himself saved together with his daughters after gaining the mountain, while his wife was turned into a pillar of salt, a monumental warning and a memorial of her wicked choice (her looking back)? So be on your guard: do not turn back to "what is behind," first "putting your hand to the plow" (Lk 9.62) and then "turning back" to the bitter savor of the things of

this world. No; flee to the mountain, to Jesus Christ, the "stone hewn without hands" (Dan 2.45) that has filled the world.

9. When you renounce Satan, trampling underfoot every covenant with him, then you annul that ancient "league with Hell," and God's paradise opens before you, that Eden, planted in the east, from which for his transgression our first father was banished. Symbolic of this is your facing about from the west to the east, the place of light. It was at this point that you were told to say: "I believe in the Father and in the Son, and in the Holy Spirit, and in one Baptism of repentance." But these subjects have been treated at large, as God's grace allowed, in the previous discourses.

10. In the security, then, of this formula of faith, "be sober." For our adversary, the devil, in the words just read, "as a roaring lion, goes about seeking whom he may devour" (1 Pet 5.8, 9). Yet if in former times Death was mighty and devoured, now, in the time of the holy laver of regeneration, the Lord God has wiped away all tears from every face" (Is 25.8). No more shall you mourn, now that you have "put off the old man" (Eph 4.22), but you shall ever keep high festival, clad in Jesus Christ as in a garment of salvation.

11. That was what was done in the outer chamber. When we enter, God willing, in the succeeding discourses on the mysteries, into the holy of holies, we shall receive the key to the rites performed there. Now to God, with the Son and the Holy Spirit, be glory, power and majesty forever and ever. Amen.

SECOND LECTURE ON THE MYSTERIES

Baptism: The Rites of the Inner Chamber

"Do you not know that all we who have been baptized into Christ Jesus have been baptized into his death? . . . since you are not under law but under grace" (Rom 6. 3–14).

1. The daily initiatory expositions, with their new teaching telling of new realities, are profitable to you, especially to those of you who have just been renewed from oldness to newness. I shall, therefore, resuming from yesterday, expound the bare essentials of

our next topic, explaining the symbolical meaning of what you did in the inner chamber.

2. Immediately, then, upon entering, you removed your tunics. This was a figure of the "stripping off of the old man with his deeds" (Col 3.9). Having stripped, you were naked, in this also imitating Christ, who was naked on the cross, by his nakedness "throwing off the cosmic powers and authorities like a garment and publicly upon the cross leading them in his triumphal procession" (Col 2.15). For as the forces of the enemy made their lair in our members, you may no longer wear the old garment. I do not, of course, refer to this visible garment, but to "the old man, which deluded by its lusts, is sinking towards death" (Eph 4.22). May the soul that has once put off that old self never again put it on, but say with the Bride of Christ in the Song of Songs: "I have put off my garment: how shall I put it on?"(Song 5.3). Marvelous! You were naked in the sight of all and were not ashamed! Truly you bore the image of the first-formed Adam, who was naked in the garden and "was not ashamed" (Gen 2.25).

3. Then, when stripped, you were anointed with exorcized olive oil from the topmost hairs of your head to the soles of your feet, and became partakers of the good olive tree, Jesus Christ. Cuttings from the wild olive tree, you were grafted into the good olive tree and became partakers of the fatness of the true olive tree. The exorcized olive oil, therefore, symbolized the partaking of the richness of Christ; its effect is to disperse every concentration of the cosmic forces arrayed against us. For as the breath of the saints upon you, with the invocation of the name of God, burns the devils like fierce fire and expels them, so this exorcized olive oil receives, through prayer and the invocation of God, power so great as not only to burn and purge away the traces of sin but also to put to rout all the invisible forces of the Evil One.

4. After this you were conducted to the sacred pool of divine Baptism, as Christ passed from the cross to the sepulchre you see before you. You were asked, one by one, whether you believed in the name of the Father and of the Son and of the Holy Spirit; you made that saving confession, and then you dipped thrice under the water and thrice rose up again, therein mystically signifying

Christ's three days' burial. For as our Savior passed three days and three nights in the bowels of the earth, so you by your first rising out of the water represented Christ's first day in the earth, and by your descent the night. For as in the night one no longer sees, while by day one is in the light, so you during your immersion, as in a night, saw nothing, but on coming up found yourselves in the day. In the same moment you were dying and being born, and that saving water was at once your grave and your mother. What Solomon said in another context is applicable to you: "A time for giving birth, a time for dying" (Eccl 3.2); although for you, contrariwise, it is a case of a time for dying and a time for being born. One time brought both, and your death coincided with your birth.

5. The strange, the extraordinary, thing is that we did not really die, nor were we really buried or really crucified; nor did we really rise again: this was figurative and symbolic; yet our salvation was real. Christ's crucifixion was real, His burial was real, and His resurrection was real; and all these He has freely made ours, that by sharing His sufferings in a symbolic enactment we may really and truly gain salvation. Oh, too generous love! Christ received the nails in His immaculate hands and feet; Christ felt the pain: and on me without pain or labor, through the fellowship of His pain, He freely bestows salvation.

6. Let no one imagine, then, that Baptism wins only the grace of remission of sins plus adoption, as John's baptism conferred only the remission of sins. No; we know full well that Baptism not only washes away our sins and procures for us the gift of the Holy Spirit, but is also the antitype of the Passion of Christ. That is why Paul just now proclaimed: "Do you not know that all we who have been baptized into Christ Jesus have been baptized into his death? For through baptism we were buried along with Him" (Rom 6.3, 4). Perhaps this was directed against those who supposed that Baptism procures only the remission of sins and the adoption of sons and does not, beyond this, really make us imitatively partakers of the sufferings of Christ.

7. To teach us, then, that all that Christ endured for us and for our salvation, He suffered in actual fact and not in mere seeming, and that we have fellowship in his passion, Paul cries aloud in unequivocal language: "For if we have become one planting with Him by the likeness of his death, we shall be one with him by the likeness of His resurrection." "One planting" is apt, for since the true vine was planted here, we, by partaking in the Baptism of his death, have become "one planting" with Him. Mark closely the words of the Apostle: he did not say: "for if we have become one planting by his death," but "by the likeness of His death." For in the case of Christ death was real, His soul being really separated from His body. His burial, too, was real, for His sacred Body was wrapped in clean linen. In His case it all really happened. But in your case there was only a likeness of death and suffering, whereas of salvation there was no likeness, but the reality.

8. That should be sufficient instruction on these points. I urge you to keep it in your memory that I too, though unworthy, may be able to say of you: "I love you because at all times you keep me in mind and maintain the tradition handed onto you. God, who has presented you as those who have come alive from the dead, is able to grant to you to walk in newness of life, because His is the glory and the power, now and forever. Amen."

THIRD LECTURE ON THE MYSTERIES

The Holy Chrism

"But you have an anointing from God and you know all things, etc. . . . that we may have confidence and may not shrink ashamed from him at his coming"(1 Jn 2.20–28).

1. "Baptized into Christ" and "clothed with Christ," you have been shaped to the likeness of the Son of God. For God, in "predestining us to be adopted as his sons" (Eph 1.5), has "conformed us to the body of the glory" (Phil 3.21) of Christ. As "partakers of Christ," therefore, you are rightly called Christs, i.e., "anointed ones": it was of you that God said: "Touch not my Christs" (Ps 105.15). Now you became Christs by receiving the antitype of the Holy Spirit; everything has been wrought in you "likewise" because you are likenesses of Christ.

He bathed in the river Jordan and, after imparting the fragrance of His Godhead to the waters, came up from them. Him the

Holy Spirit visited in essential presence, like resting upon like. Similarly for you, after you had ascended from the sacred streams, there was an anointing with chrism, the antitype of that with which Christ was anointed, that is, of the Holy Spirit. Concerning the Spirit the blessed Isaiah, in the prophetical book which bears his name said, speaking in the person of the Lord: "The Spirit of the Lord is upon me because he hath anointed me. He hath sent me to preach glad tidings to the poor" (Is 61.1).

2. For Christ was not anointed with material oil or balsam; His Father, appointing Him Savior of the whole world, anointed Him with the Holy Spirit as Peter says: "Jesus of Nazareth, whom God anointed with the Holy Spirit" (Acts 10.38). The prophet David also made proclamation: "Thy throne, God, is forever and ever: the scepter of thy kingdom is a scepter of uprightness. You have loved justice, and hated iniquity: therefore God, thy God, hath anointed thee with the oil of gladness above thy fellows" (Ps 45.7).

As Christ was really crucified and buried and rose again, and you at Baptism are privileged to be crucified, buried, and raised along with Him in a likeness, so also with the chrism. Christ was anointed with a mystical oil of gladness; that is, with the Holy Spirit, called oil of gladness because he is the cause of spiritual gladness; so you, being anointed with ointment, have become partakers and fellows of Christ.

3. Beware of supposing that this ointment is mere ointment. Just as after the invocation of the Holy Spirit the Eucharistic bread is no longer ordinary bread, but the body of Christ, so this holy oil, in conjunction with the invocation, is no longer simple or common oil, but becomes the gracious gift of Christ and the Holy Spirit, producing the advent of His deity. With this ointment your forehead and sense organs are sacramentally anointed, in such wise that while your body is anointed with the visible oil, your soul is sanctified by the holy, quickening Spirit.

4. You are anointed first upon the forehead to rid you of the shame which the first human transgressor bore about with him everywhere; so you may "reflect as in a glass the splendor of the Lord" (2 Cor 3.18). Then upon the ears, to receive ears quick to hear the divine mysteries, the ears of which Isaiah said: "The Lord

gave me also an ear to hear," and the Lord Jesus in the Gospels: "He who has ears to hear, let him hear" (Mt 11.15). Then upon the nostrils, that, scenting the divine oil, you may say: "We are the incense offered by Christ to God, in the case of those who are on the way to salvation" (2 Cor 2.15). Then on the breast, that "putting on the breastplate of justice you may be able to withstand the wiles of the Devil" (Eph 6.14). For as Christ after his baptism and the visitation of the Holy Spirit went forth and overthrew the adversary, so must you after holy Baptism and the mystical Chrism, clad in the armor of the Holy Spirit, stand firm against the forces of the Enemy who overthrow them, saying: "I can do all things in the Christ who strengthens me" (Phil 4.13).

5. Once privileged to receive the holy Chrism, you are called Christians and have a name that bespeaks your new birth. Before admission to Baptism and the grace of the Holy Spirit you were not strictly entitled to this name but were like people on the way toward being Christians.

6. You must know that this Chrism is prefigured in the Old Testament. When Moses, conferring on his brother the divine appointment, was ordering him high priest, he anointed him after he had bathed in water, and henceforward he was called "Christ" ["anointed"], clearly after the figurative chrism. Again, the high priest, when installing Solomon as king, anointed him after he had bathed in Gihon. But what was done to them in figure was done to you, not in figure but in truth, because your salvation began from Him who was anointed by the Holy Spirit in truth. Christ is the beginning of your salvation, since He is truly the first handful of dough and you the "whole lump": and if the first handful be holy, plainly its holiness will permeate the lump.

7. Keep this Chrism unsullied: for it shall teach you all things if it abide in you, as you heard the blessed John declaring just now as he expatiated upon the Chrism. For this holy thing is both a heavenly protection for the body and salvation for the soul. It was of this anointing that in ancient times the blessed Isaiah prophesied saying: "And the Lord shall make unto all people in this mountain" (elsewhere also he calls the Church a mountain, as when he says: "And in the last days the mountain of the Lord shall

be manifest" (Is 2.2), ". . . and they shall drink wine, they shall drink gladness, they shall anoint themselves with ointment." To alert you to the mystical meaning of "ointment" here, he says: "All this deliver to the nations: for the counsel of the Lord is upon all the nations" (Is 25.7). Anointed, then, with this holy oil, keep it in you unsullied, without blame, making progress through good works and becoming well-pleasing to "the trail-blazer of our salvation" (Heb 2.10), Christ Jesus, to whom be glory forever and ever. Amen.

FOURTH LECTURE ON THE MYSTERIES

The Eucharist (I): The Body and Blood of Christ

"For I myself received from the Lord the traditions which in turn I passed on to you. . . ." (1 Cor 11.23)

1. The teaching of blessed Paul is of itself sufficient to give you full assurance about the divine mysteries by admission to which you have become one body and blood with Christ. For Paul just now proclaimed ". . . that on the night in which he was betrayed our Lord Jesus Christ took bread and, after giving thanks, broke it, and gave it to his disciples saying, "Take, eat: this is my body;" then, taking the cup, he gave thanks and said, "Take, drink: this is my blood" (1 Cor 11.23, 24). When the Master himself has explicitly said of the bread, "This is my body," will anyone still dare to doubt? When He is Himself our warranty, saying, "This is my blood," who will ever waver and say it is not His blood?

2. Once at Cana in Galilee, He changed water into wine by His sovereign will; is it not credible, then, that He changed wine into blood? If as a guest at a physical marriage He performed this stupendous miracle, shall He not far more readily be confessed to have bestowed on "the friends of the bridegroom" the fruition of His own Body and Blood?

3. With perfect confidence, then, we partake as of the Body and Blood of Christ. For in the figure of bread His Body is given to you, and in the figure of wine His Blood, that partaking of the Body and Blood of Christ you may become of one body and blood

with him. For when His Body and Blood become the tissue of our members, we become Christ-bearers, and as the blessed Peter said, "Partakers of the divine nature" (2 Pet 1.4).

4. Once, speaking to the Jews, Christ said: "Unless you eat my flesh and drink my blood, you can have no life in you." Not understanding His words spiritually, they "were shocked and drew back," imagining that He was proposing the eating of human flesh.

5. The Old Covenant had its loaves of proposition, but they, as belonging to the Covenant, have come to an end. The New Covenant has its heavenly bread and cup of salvation, to sanctify both body and soul. For as the bread is for the body, the Word suits the soul.

6. Do not then think of the elements as bare bread and wine; they are, according to the Lord's declaration, the Body and Blood of Christ. Though sense suggests the contrary, let faith be your stay. Instead of judging matters by taste, let faith give you an unwavering confidence that you have been privileged to receive the Body and Blood of Christ.

7. The blessed David is hinting to you the meaning of these rites when he says, "You have prepared a table before me, against those who oppress me" (Ps 23.5). What he means is this: "Before your coming the devils prepared a table for mankind, a table defiled and polluted, impregnated with diabolical power; but since your coming, Lord, you have prepared a table in my presence." When man says to God, "You have prepared a table before me," what else does he refer to but the mystical and spiritual table which God has prepared for us "over against," meaning "arrayed against and opposed to," the evil spirits? And very aptly: for that table gave communion with devils while this gives communion with God.

"You have anointed my head with oil" (Ex 28.36). He has anointed your head with oil upon your forehead, meaning the seal which you have of God, that you may be made "the engraving of the signet," that is, the sanctuary of God.

"Your chalice, also, which inebriates me, how goodly is it!" (Ps 22.5). You see here spoken of the chalice which Jesus took in his hands and of which, after giving thanks, he said: "This is my blood shed for many for the forgiveness of sins."

8. For this reason Solomon also, in **Ecclesiastes** overtly alluding to this grace, says: "Come hither, eat your bread with joy" (Eccl 9.7, 8), that is, the mystical bread. "Come hither," he calls: a saving, beatific call. "And drink your wine with a merry heart": that is, the mystical wine. "And let oil be poured out upon your head": you see how he hints also of the mystical chrism. "And at all times let your garments be white, because the Lord approves what you do." It is now that the Lord approves what you do; for before you came to the grace your doings were "vanity of vanities" (Eccl 1.2).

Now that you have put off your old garments and put on those which are spiritually white, you must go clad in white all your days. I do not, of course, mean that your ordinary clothes must always be white, but that you must be clad in those true, spiritual garments which are white and shining. Then you will be able to say with the blessed Isaiah: "Let my soul rejoice in the Lord, for he has dressed me in the garments of salvation, and with the robe of gladness he has clothed me" (Is 61.10).

9. In this knowledge, and in the firm conviction that the bread which is seen is not bread, though it is bread to the taste, but the Body of Christ, and that the visible wine is not wine, though taste will have it so, but the Blood of Christ; and that it was of this that David sang of old: "Bread strengthens the heart of man, soon his face glistens joyously with oil" (Ps 103.15), strengthen your heart, partaking of this Bread as spiritual, and make cheerful the face of your soul. God grant that, your soul's face unveiled with a clear conscience, you may "reflecting as in a glass the glory of the Lord," go "from glory to glory" in Christ Jesus our Lord, whose is the glory for ever and ever. Amen.

FIFTH LECTURE ON THE MYSTERIES

The Eucharist (II): The Liturgy

"Laying aside, then, all malice, deceit and slander" etc. (1 Pet 2.1).

1.   By the mercy of God you have in our former assemblies received sufficient instruction about Baptism, Chrism, and the partaking of the Body and Blood of Christ. We must now pass on to the next subject, intending today to crown the work of your spiritual edification.

The Hand Washing

2.   You saw the deacon who offers the water for the washing of hands to the celebrant and to the presbyters who encircle the altar of God. Not that he offered this water on account of any bodily uncleanness: of course not; for we did not originally enter the church unwashed. No; the ablution is a symbolic action, a symbol of our obligation to be clean from all sins and transgressions. The hands symbolize action; so by washing them we signify evidently the purity and blamelessness of our conduct. Did you not hear the blessed David supplying the key to this ceremony in the divine mysteries when he says: "I will wash my hands among the innocent: and will circle thy altar, O Lord"? (Ps 25.6). The hand washing, then, is a symbol of innocence.

The Kiss

3.   Next the deacon cries: "Welcome one another," and "Let us kiss one another." You must not suppose that kiss is the kiss customarily exchanged in the streets by ordinary friends. This kiss is different, effecting, as it does, a commingling of souls and mutually pledging unreserved forgiveness. The kiss, then, is a sign of a true union of hearts, banishing every grudge. It was this that Christ had in view when He said: "If, when you are bringing your gift to the altar, you suddenly remember that your brother has a grievance against you, leave your offering by the altar; first go and make your peace with your brother and then come back and offer your gift" (Mt 5.23). The kiss, then, is a reconciliation and therefore holy, as the blessed Paul said somewhere when he commanded us to "salute one another with a holy kiss" (1 Cor 16.20) and Peter: "Salute one another with a kiss of charity" (1 Pet 5:14).

4.   Then the celebrant cries: "Lift up your hearts." For truly it is right in that most awful hour to have one's heart on high with

God, not below, occupied with earth and the things of earth. In effect, then, the bishop commands everyone to banish worldly thoughts and workaday cares and to have their hearts in heaven with the good God.

Assenting, you answer, "We have them lifted up to the Lord." Let no one present be so disposed that while his lips form the words, "We have them lifted up to the Lord," in his mind his attention is engaged by worldly thoughts. At times we should commemorate God, but at least, if this is not possible to human weakness, we must aspire to it in that hour.

5. Then the priest says: "Let us give thanks to the Lord." Indeed we ought to give thanks to the Lord for calling us, when we were unworthy, to so great a grace, for reconciling us when we were enemies, and for vouchsafing to us the spirit of adoption.

Then you say: "It is meet and just." In giving thanks we do indeed a meet thing and a just; but He did, not a just thing, but one that went beyond justice, in deigning to bestow on us such marvelous blessings.

Memorial of Creation: Sanctus

6. After that we commemorate the heavens, the earth and the sea; the sun and moon, the stars, the whole rational and irrational creation, both visible and invisible: Angels and Archangels; Virtues, Dominions, Principalities, Powers, Thrones and the many-faced Cherubim: equivalently saying with David, "O magnify the Lord with me." We commemorate also the Seraphim whom Isaiah in the Holy Spirit saw encircling the throne of God, "with two wings veiling their faces and with two their feet, while with two they did fly," as they chanted: "Holy, Holy, Holy, Lord of Hosts" (Is 6.2, 3). It is to mingle our voices in the hymns of the heavenly armies that we recite this doxology which descends to us from the Seraphim.

Epiclesis and Consecration

7. Next, after sanctifying ourselves by these spiritual songs, we implore the merciful God to send forth His Holy Spirit upon the offering to make the bread the Body of Christ and the wine the

Blood of Christ. For whatever the Holy Spirit touches is hallowed and changed.

The Intercession

8. Next, when the spiritual sacrifice, the bloodless worship, has been completed, over that sacrifice of propitiation we beseech God for the public peace of the Churches, for the good estate of the world, for the Emperors, for the armed forces and our allies, for those in sickness, for the distressed: for all, in a word, who need help, we all pray and offer this sacrifice.

9. Then we commemorate also those who have fallen asleep: first of all, the patriarchs, prophets, apostles, and martyrs, that God through their intercessory prayers may accept our supplication. Next we pray also for the holy Fathers and Bishops who have fallen asleep, and generally for all who have gone before us, believing that this will be the greatest benefit to the souls of those on whose behalf our supplication is offered in the presence of the holy, the most dread Sacrifice.

10. Let me use an illustration for an argument. For I know that many of you say: "What does it avail a soul departing this world, whether with or without sins, to be remembered at the Sacrifice?" Well, suppose a king banished persons who had offended him, and then their relatives wove a garland and presented it to him on behalf of those undergoing punishment, would he not mitigate their sentence? In the same way, offering our supplication to Him for those who have fallen asleep, even though they be sinners, we, though we weave no garland, offer Christ slain for our sins, propitiating the merciful God on both their and our own behalf.

The Lord's Prayer

11. Then, after this, we recite that prayer which the Savior delivered to His own disciples, with a clear conscience designating God as our Father, saying: "Our Father, who art in heaven."

The Communion

19. Next the priest says: "Holy things to the holy." Holy are the offerings after they have received the visitation of the Holy Spirit; and you are holy after you have been privileged to receive the Holy Spirit. So things and persons correspond: both are holy. Next you say: "One is holy, one is the Lord, Jesus Christ." For truly One only is holy—holy that is, by nature; yet we also are holy, not, indeed, by nature, but by participation, training and prayer.

20. After this you hear the chanter inviting you with a sacred melody to communion in the holy mysteries, in the words: "O taste and see that the Lord is good" (Ps 34.9). Entrust not your judgment to your bodily palate, but to unwavering faith. For in tasting you taste, not bread and wine, but the antitypical Body and Blood of Christ.

21. Coming up to receive, therefore, do not approach with your wrists extended or your fingers splayed, but making your left hand a throne for the right (for it is about to receive a King) and cupping your palm, so receive the Body of Christ; and answer: "Amen." Carefully hallow your eyes by the touch of the sacred Body, and then partake, taking care to lose no part of it. Such a loss would be like a mutilation of your own body. Why, if you had been given gold dust, would you not take the utmost care to hold it fast, not letting a grain slip through your fingers, lest you be by so much the poorer? How much more carefully, then, will you guard against losing so much as a crumb of that which is more precious than gold or precious stones!

22. After partaking of the Body of Christ, approach also the chalice of His Blood. Do not stretch out your hands, but bowing low in a posture of worship and reverence as you say, "Amen," sanctify yourself by receiving also the Blood of Christ. While it is still warm upon your lips, moisten your finger with It and so sanctify your eyes, your forehead, and other organs of sense. Then wait for the prayer and give thanks to the God who has deigned to admit you to such high mysteries.

23. Preserve this traditional teaching untarnished; keep yourselves unsullied by sin. Never cut yourselves off from the fellowship [communion], never through the pollution of sin deprive yourselves of these sacred, spiritual mysteries. "And may the God of peace sanctify you completely, and may your whole spirit, soul and body be preserved blameless at the coming of our Lord Jesus Christ" (1 Thes 5.23), whose is the glory now and evermore, world without end. Amen.

CHAPTER TWELVE

JOHN CHRYSOSTOM

John Chrysostom was born in Antioch of Syria about 347. He was baptized in 370 after studies in the school of the rhetorician Libanius. After his baptism he took up the life of a monk and hermit, but the very intensity with which he took up this form of life compelled him to leave and return to Antioch, where he was ordained a priest in 386. His brilliant gifts as a preacher, moralist, and exegete of the Antiochean school of literal interpretation led to his elevation to the patriarchate of Constantinople in 397. He so angered Theophilus of Alexandria that an illegal synod convoked by Theophilus deposed him from his see in absentia. With the cooperation of the Empress Eudoxia, whose wrath Chrysostom had previously aroused, Theophilus successfully pressed for his exile. The people of Constantinople threatened to riot and he was immediately recalled. He was subsequently sent into exile, from which he did not return, once again in 404. He was first exiled to Cucusus in Armenia. There he kept in touch by letter with the people of Constantinople and was able to receive visitors from the city, but he was later ordered to a more remote place of exile, Pityus, 600 miles across the Black Sea. The trip into exile had to be made overland and Chrysostom did not survive the rigors of the trip. He died on September 14, 407, three years after he left Constantinople, with the words, "Glory to God for all things!" on his lips.

In 1955 a complete series of Chrysostom's catechetical instructions, previously unknown, was discovered. Given Chrysostom's renown as an orator of such skill that his audience would interrupt him with applause, shouts of admiration, and tears of repentance, the discovery was immediately recognized to be of outstanding importance to sacramental theologians and historians of the liturgy.

Unlike the sermons of Ambrose of Milan and Cyril of Jerusalem, which were directed to the newly baptized in the week following Easter, the "Second Instruction" of Chrysostom, reproduced here, was directed to the catechumens of Antioch, about the year C.E.390 during the

119

Lenten period of preparation. The "Instruction" is particularly rich in the description of the rites of initiation as it was conferred in that city at the end of the fourth century. It both confirms what we know of the rites from other sources, such as Theodore of Mopsuestia and Cyril, and sheds new light on them.

Of particular interest in the following "Instruction" is his explanation of the rite of exorcism, his address to the sponsors of the catechumens, and his description of the renunciation of Satan followed by profession of adherence to Christ, the prebaptismal anointings and the sacramental formula used in the conferral of baptism. There is no description of a separate anointing or imposition of hands symbolizing the gift of the Holy Spirit, whose descent upon the neophyte is associated with the moment of baptism itself. Chrysostom concludes with a touching description of the joyful reception of the newly baptized by all who are present. They are then immediately conducted into the church where they will participate for the first time in the celebration of the Eucharist.

[Translation: ACW, 31, pp. 43–55]

THE SECOND INSTRUCTION

A Continuation to Those Who Are About to Be Baptized and a Clear Explanation of What Is Accomplished in a Symbolic and Figurative Fashion in Holy Baptism

1. Again let me address a few words to those who have enlisted in Christ's special army; let me show them the power of the weapons they are about to receive and the ineffable good which a kindly God displays for the race of men, so that they may come forward with great faith and full assurance and enjoy the honor He bestows in greater abundance. From the very outset, beloved, consider how great is the goodness God has shown to us. In His judgment, even those who have never suffered and who have given no evidence of any excellence deserve this great gift, and He forgives the sins they have committed during their whole past. In view of the great honor He bestows, you should dispose your hearts well and be willing to contribute your fair share. If you do so, how generous a recompense do you think the loving God will deem that you deserve?

2. No one has ever seen the like of this in human dealings. In fact, many a man has many a time submitted to many troubles and miseries in the hope of a reward, but he has come home with empty hands. Why? Either the men from whom he expected a reward turned out to be ungrateful to him despite his many toils, or death, like as not, snatched him from our midst before his time and, hence he failed to satisfy his aim. But in the service of our Master we can suspect no such failure. Even before we have begun to suffer or to prove our worth, He anticipates our response and shows us the honor He bestows. Thus his many favors move us to look to our own salvation.

God's Action with Regard to the First Man

3. In this way, then, did God from the very beginning constantly show kindness to the human race. For as soon as He created the first man, He straightway and from the first settled him in Paradise, granted him that gift of a carefree life, and offered him the enjoyment of everything in Paradise except one tree. Because he wished to indulge his taste, and because his wife misled him, he trampled underfoot the command which God had imposed on him and committed an outrage against the great honor which God had bestowed on him.

4. But see even here the magnitude of God's kindness. For God no longer had to judge worthy of any forgiveness one who had proved so ungrateful for unearned benefactions, but He should have put him beyond the pale of His providence. But he did not do so. Not only that but, like a loving Father who is moved by his natural affection for his unruly child, He does not measure His rebuke to the sin nor, again, does he forgive altogether but he punishes him with moderation, so that the child, like a ship, may not thereafter run aground on a reef of greater evil. That is the way in which God works. Since man had shown great disobedience, God cast him forth from his life in Paradise. God curbed man's spirit for the future, so that he might not leap any further away, and He condemned him to a life of toil and labor, speaking to him in some such fashion as this:

5. "The ease and security which were yours in abundance have led you to this great disobedience. They made you forget my commandments. You had nothing to do, that led you to think thoughts too haughty for your own nature, ' . . . for idleness hath taught all evil' (Eccl 33.29). Therefore, I condemn you to toil and labor so that while tilling the earth, you may never forget your disobedience and the vileness of your nature. Since you exalted yourself to great heights and refused to remain within your proper bounds, on this account do I command you to return again to the dust from which you were taken, ' . . . for dust thou art, and into dust thou shalt return'" (Gen 3.19).

6. To increase man's pain and to make him feel his fall to the full, God did not settle man at any great distance from Paradise, but nearby. However, He blocked off the entrance to it, so that man might see each hour the joys of which he had deprived himself by his failure to obey; thus might man profit from this constant admonition and in the future be more careful to keep the commandments God had given to him. When we enjoy blessings without perceiving the manner of the benefaction as we should, and then are deprived of them, we get a fuller perception of these blessings, and we also endure a greater pain of loss. This is what happened in the case of the first man.

7. But that you may know both the plot of the wicked demon and the wise provisions of our Master, consider what the devil tried to make of man by his deceit and what kindness our Master and Protector showed for him. For that wicked one, the devil, envied man his life in Paradise and, by the prospect of a greater promise, he drove him forth from the blessings which were in his hands. For by making man picture himself as equal to God, he drove him to the punishment of death. Such are his wiles that he not only drives us away from the blessings we have, but he also tries to drive us onto a more precipitous cliff. But God in His love did not fail to regard mankind. He showed the devil how foolish were his attempts; He showed man the great care He manifested in his regard, for through death He gave man everlasting life. The devil drove man from Paradise; God led him to heaven. The profit is greater than the loss.

8. But as I said in the beginning—and it was on this account that I was induced to talk about these matters—God judged worthy of His own great kindness a man who turned out to be ungrateful for these great benefactions. If you, the soldiers of Christ, will show your eagerness to be grateful for these ineffable gifts which are coming to you, if you will be alert to guard those which have already come, what great munificence will you win from Him for having guarded His gifts well? For it is the Master who said: "To everyone who has shall be given, and he shall have abundance" (Mt 25.29). For the man who proves himself worthy of the gifts already received, would deserve to enjoy greater gifts.

See with the Eyes of Faith

9. All of you, then, who have deserved to be enrolled in this heavenly book, bring forward a generous faith and a strong reason. What takes place here requires faith and the eyes of the soul, so that you pay heed not only to what is seen, but that you make the unseen visible from the seen. This is what the eyes of faith can do. The eyes of the body can only see what comes under their perception, but the eyes of faith are quite the opposite. For they see nothing of visible things, but the invisible things they see as if they were lying before their eyes. This is faith: to see the invisible as if it were visible. St. Paul says: "Now faith is the substance of things to be hoped for, the evidence of things that are not seen" (Heb 11.1).

10. What is this I am saying and why did I say to pay no heed to visible things, but to have the eyes of the spirit? I say it in order that when you see the bath of water and the hand of the priest touching your head, you may not think that this is merely water, not that only the hand of the bishop lies upon your head. For it is not a man who does what is done, but it is the grace of the Spirit which sanctifies the nature of the water and touches your head together with the hand of the priest. Was I not right in saying that we need the eyes of faith? With these we believe in the invisible; with these we take no notice of what can be seen.

11. Baptism is a burial and a resurrection. For the old man is buried with his sin and the new man is resurrected, being resurrected according to the image of his Creator. We put off the old garment, which has been made filthy with the abundance of our sins; we put on the new one, which is free from every stain. What am I saying? We put on Christ Himself. "For all of you," says St. Paul, "who have been baptized into Christ, have put on Christ" (Gal 3.27).

Purpose and Symbolism of the Exorcisms

12. Now you stand at the threshold; soon you will enjoy the benefit of so many gifts. Let me instruct you, then, as far as I can, in the reasons for each of the present rites, that you may know them well and depart from here with a more certain understanding of them. You must understand why, after this daily instruction, we send you along to hear the word of the exorcists. For this rite does not take place without aim or purpose; you are going to receive the King of heaven to dwell within you. This is why, after we have admonished you, those appointed to this task take you and, as if they were preparing for a royal visit, they cleanse your minds by those awesome words, putting to flight every device of the wicked one and making your hearts worthy of the royal presence. For even if the demon be fierce and cruel, he must withdraw from your hearts with all speed after this awesome formula and the invocation of the common Master of all things. Along with this, the rite itself impresses great piety on the soul and leads it to abundant compunction.

13. It is certainly marvelous and contrary to expectation, but this rite does away with all difference and distinction of rank. Even if a man happens to enjoy worldly honor, if he happens to glitter with wealth, if he boasts of high lineage or the glory which is his in this world, he stands side by side with the beggar and with him who is clothed in rags, and many a time with the blind and the lame. Nor is he disgusted by this, because he knows that all these differences find no place in the world of the spirit, where one looks only for a soul that is well disposed.

14. See what profit those words and those awesome and wonderful invocations bring with them! But the show of bare feet and the outstretched hands point out something else to us. Those who endure captivity of the body show by their posture their dejection at the disaster which has overcome them. So, too, when the devil's captives are about to be set free from his domination and to come under the yoke of goodness, they first remind themselves of their prior condition by their external attitude. They do this that they may be able to know from what evil they are being delivered and to what good they are hurrying, and that this very knowledge may be the foundation for greater gratitude and may make their souls even more than well disposed.

Address to the Sponsors

15. Do you wish me to address a word to those who are sponsoring you, that they too may know what recompense they deserve if they have shown great care for you, and what condemnation follows if they are careless? Consider, beloved, how those who go surety for someone in a matter of money set themselves a greater risk than the one who borrows the money and is liable for it. If the borrower be well disposed, he lightens the burden for his surety; if the dispositions of his soul be ill, he makes the risk a steeper one. Wherefore, the wise man counsels us, saying: "If thou be surety, think as if thou wert to pay it" (Eccl 8.16). If, then, those who go surety for others in a matter of money make themselves liable for the whole sum, those who go surety for others in matters of the spirit and on an account which involves virtue should be much more alert. They ought to show their paternal love by encouraging, counseling, and correcting those for whom they go surety.

16. Let them not think that what takes place is a trifling thing, but let them see clearly that they share in the credit if by their admonition they lead those entrusted to them to the path of virtue. Again, if those they sponsor become careless, the sponsors themselves will suffer great punishment. That is why it is customary to call the sponsors "spiritual fathers," that they may learn by this very action how great an affection they must show to those they sponsor in the matter of spiritual instruction. If it is a noble thing to lead to a zeal for virtue those who are in no way related to us, much more should we fulfill this precept in the case of the one whom we receive as a spiritual son. You, the sponsors, have learned that no slight danger hangs over your heads if you are remiss.

The Renouncement of Satan and Adherence to Christ

17. Now let me speak to you of the mysteries themselves and of the contract which will be made between yourselves and the Master. In worldly affairs, whenever someone wishes to entrust his business to anyone, a written contract must be completed between the trustee and his client. The same thing holds true now, when the Master is going to entrust to you not mortal things which are subject to destruction and death, but spiritual things which belong to eternity. Wherefore, this contract is also called faith, since it possesses nothing visible but all things which can be seen by the eyes of the spirit. There must be an agreement between the contracting parties. However, it is not on paper nor written in ink; it is in God and written by the Spirit. The words which you utter here are registered in heaven, and the agreement you make by your tongue abides indelibly with the Master.

18. See here again the external attitude of captivity. The priests bring you in. First they bid you to pray on bent knees, with your hands outstretched to heaven, and to remind yourselves by your posture from what evil you are delivered and to what good you will dedicate yourselves. Then the priest comes to you one by one, asks for your contract and confession, and prepares you to utter those awesome and frightening words; "I renounce thee, Satan."

19. Now tears and bitter groans assail me. For I thought of the day on which I too was judged worthy to speak those words. When I consider the burden of sins I have accumulated from that day to this, my mind is confounded; my reason is cut to the quick when I see what shame I have poured on myself by my subsequent negligence. Wherefore, I beg all of you to show some generosity to me, especially since you are about to meet the King. He will receive you with great eagerness; He will put upon you that royal robe; He will give you gifts, as many as you wish and of whatever kind you wish, but only if we ask for spiritual things. Ask for a grace in my behalf, that He may not demand from me an accounting for my sins, but granting me pardon, He may hereafter judge me worthy of His favor. I do not doubt that you will do this, because you show a deep affection for those who teach you.

20. Now let us get back to the sequence of our discourse. Then the priest has you say: "I renounce thee, Satan, thy pomps, thy service, and thy works." The words are few but their power is great. The angels who are standing by and the invisible powers rejoice at your conversion, receive the words from your tongues, and carry them up to the common Master of all things. They are inscribed in the books of heaven.

21. Did you see what the terms of the agreement are? After the renunciation of the wicked one and of all things which are important to him, the priest again has you say: "And I enter thy service, O Christ." Did you see his boundless goodness? Receiving only these words from you, He entrusts to you such a store of treasures! He has forgotten all your former ingratitude, He reminds you of none of your past deeds, but He is content with these few words.

Anointing of the Catechumens and Their Baptism

22. After that contract of renunciation and attachment, after you have confessed His sovereignty and by the words you spoke have attached yourself to Christ, in the next place, as if you were a combatant chosen for the spiritual arena, the priest anoints you on the forehead with the oil of the Spirit and signs you [with the sign of the cross], saying: "So-and-so is anointed in the name of the Father, and of the Son, and of the Holy Spirit."

23. The priest knows that henceforth the enemy is furious, grinds his teeth, and goes about like a roaring lion when he sees those who were formerly subject to his sovereignty in sudden rebellion against him, but going over to the side of Christ. Therefore, the priest anoints you on the forehead and puts on you the sign [of the cross], in order that the enemy may turn away his eyes. For he does not dare look you in the face when he sees the lightning flash which leaps forth from it and blinds his eyes. Henceforth from that day there is strife and counterstrife with him, and on this account the priest leads you into the spiritual arena as athletes of Christ by virtue of this anointing.

24. Next after this, in the full darkness of the night, he strips off your robe and, as if he were going to lead you into heaven itself by the ritual, he causes your whole body to be anointed with that olive oil of the spirit, so that all your limbs may be fortified and unconquered by the darts which the adversary aims at you.

25. After this anointing the priest makes you go down into the sacred waters, burying the old man and at the same time raising up the new, who is renewed in the image of his Creator. It is at this moment that, through the word and the hand of the priest, the Holy Spirit descends upon you. Instead of the man who descended into the water, a different man comes forth, one who has wiped away all the filth of his sins, who has put off the old garment of sin and has put on the royal robe.

26. That you may also learn from this that the substance of the Father, Son, and Holy Spirit is one, baptism is conferred in the following manner. When the priest says: "So-and-so is baptized in the name of the Father, and of the Son, and of the Holy Spirit," he puts your head down into the water three times and three times he lifts it up again, preparing you by this mystic rite to receive the descent of the Spirit. For it is not only the priest who touches the head, but also the right hand of Christ, and this is shown by the very words of the one baptizing. He does not say: "I baptize so-and-so, but rather so-and-so is baptized," showing that he is only the minister of grace and merely offers his hand because he has been ordained to this end by the Spirit. The one fulfilling all things is the Father and the Son and the Holy Spirit, the undivided Trinity. It is faith in this Trinity which gives the remission from sin; it is this confession which gives to us the gift of filial adoption.

27. What follows suffices to show us from what those who have been judged worthy of this mystic rite have been set free, and what they have gained. As soon as they come forth from those sacred waters, all who are present embrace them, greet them, kiss them, rejoice with them, and congratulate them, because those who were heretofore slaves and captives have suddenly become free men and sons and have been invited to the royal table. For straightway after they come up from the waters, they are led to the awesome table heavy laden with countless favors, where they taste of the Master's body and blood, and become a dwelling place for the Holy Spirit. Since they have put on Christ Himself, wherever they go they are like angels on earth, rivaling the brilliance of the rays of the sun.

Closing Address: Petitions and Prayers

28. It was not idly or without purpose that I anticipated the event and instructed your loving assembly in all these matters, but I did so that you might be carried on by the wings of hope and enjoy the pleasure before you enjoyed the actual benefit. I did it, too, that you might adopt a purpose worthy of the rite, and as blessed Paul has exhorted, you might "mind the things that are above" (Col 3.2), and change your thoughts from earth to heaven, from visible things to those which are unseen. And we see the objects of bodily sight more clearly with the eyes of the spirit.

29. But since you stand at the threshold of the royal palace and are about to approach the very throne where sits the King who apportions the gifts, show every ambition in your requests. Only ask for nothing worldly or human; make your petition worthy of Him who grants gifts. As you come forth from the waters, symbolizing your resurrection by rising up from them, ask Him to be your ally, so that you may guard well the gifts He has given you, and that you may not be conquered by the deceits of the wicked one. Beg Him for peace among the churches, beseech Him for those who are being led astray, prostrate yourselves in behalf of those who are in sin, so that we may be judged worthy of mercy in some degree. For he has granted you great confidence. He has enrolled you in the front rank of His friends, and has received you into the adoption of sons , you who were formerly captives and slaves with no right to speak out. He will not reject your prayers; again imitating in this His own goodness, He will grant you everything you ask.

30. It is especially in this way that you draw Him to care for your fellow members and taking such thought for the salvation of others, He will judge that on this account you deserve to speak out with great confidence. Nothing gladdens Him so much as our fellow feeling for those who are members of the same Body, our manifestation of abundant affection for our brothers, and our great preoccupation with the salvation of our neighbors.

31. In this knowledge, then, my beloved, make yourselves ready to receive this grace with joy and gladness of spirit, that you may enjoy the abundant benefits of this gift. May all of us together, by making our conduct worthy of the grace, deserve to receive eternal and ineffable gifts by the grace and love of our Lord Jesus Christ, with whom be to the Father and Holy Spirit, glory, power, and honor, now and forever, world without end. Amen.

CHAPTER THIRTEEN

THE *DE SACRAMENTIS* OF ST. AMBROSE OF MILAN

Ambrose was born in or about C.E. 339 in Trier, a northern capital of the Roman Empire. At the age of thirty he was placed in charge of the province of Amelia Liguria and took up residence in Milan in northern Italy. The bishop of Milan had been Auxentius, an Arian, who died in 374. A dispute arose concerning his successor and Ambrose was called upon to keep the peace. To his surprise and embarrassment he was elected to succeed Auxentius even though he had not yet been baptized. His episcopacy was long and Ambrose was frequently embroiled in controversy, particularly with the royal family. He refused Justina, the Emperor's mother, permission for the use of one of the basilicas in Milan by her fellow Arians. Later he was to do battle with the Emperor Theodosius by demanding that he do public penance for the slaughter of thousands of citizens who had rioted at Thessalonica. He was just as fearless in dealing with the Pope, Damasus. Ambrose was far more than a tough-minded ecclesiastic. He had significant influence on the development of Western theological thought. He studied the Greek Fathers and assimilated much of their teaching into his own work. He won the admiration of Augustine and eventually baptized him.

The six homilies which make up the **De Sacramentis** *were probably preached on the six days following Easter in the year 391. Ambrose's bold use of the allegorical method of interpreting Scripture, which he probably absorbed from his study of the Alexandrian, Origen, has little appeal in our age with our far more critical standards of interpretation, and much of that interpretation has been omitted in the selections given below. The* **De Sacramentis** *is one of two works of post-baptismal instructions composed by Ambrose for the neophytes of Milan. The other work, the* **De Mysteriis**, *is less detailed in its description of the rites of initiation and for that reason it is the* **De Sacramentis** *which are given here.*

131

The sermons I, I–II, 7, treat of rites antecedent to the rite of baptism; the "Ephetha," anointing, renunciation of Satan, the profession of faith in the Trinity, as well as the rite of baptism itself. Of particular interest is the description of the meaning of baptism in Pauline terms of death-resurrection and Ambrose's defense of the Milanese rite of the washing of the feet of the neophytes. As Ambrose points out, this rite was not practiced in Rome, "whose character and form we follow in all things" (III, 5), but Ambrose, who does not wish to criticize the Roman procedure, is nonetheless careful to defend the Milanese ritual by appealing to the example of Jesus himself on the occasion of the Last Supper. The concluding rite of initiation prior to the celebration of the Eucharist is the invocation and conferral of the Holy Spirit. In Ambrose's description of the Eucharist, it is the repetition of the words of Christ, as distinct from the words of the Eucharistic Prayer of the priest, which effects the real presence of the Body and Blood of Christ. Finally, the prayers (IV, 21, 22, 27) before and after the consecration appear in very similar words in the present Roman Canon, our Eucharistic Prayer I, though with interesting differences.

*The selections below are, with some paragraphs of scriptural interpretation omitted, from the first four of the six homilies which make up the **De Sacramentis**. The last two, which treat of the reception of Communion and of the Lord's Prayer, are omitted.*
[Translation: FC, 44, pp. 269–307]

THE SACRAMENTS: I

1. I approach a sermon on the sacraments which you have received, whose scope should not have been presented to you before. For in the Christian man faith is first. Thus, even in Rome they are called "the faithful" who have been baptized, and our father Abraham was justified by faith, not by works. So you have received baptism, you have believed. Surely it is unfitting that I consider anything else; for you would not have been called to grace if Christ had not judged you worthy of His grace.

2. What have we done on the Sabbath? "The opening," of course. These mysteries of "the opening" were celebrated when the priest touched your ears and nostrils. What does this signify? In the

Gospel, our Lord Jesus Christ, when the deaf and dumb man was presented to Him, touched his ears and his mouth: the ears, because he was deaf, the mouth, because he was dumb. And He said: "**Effetha**" (Mk 7.34). This is a Hebrew word, which in Latin means *Adaperire* (Open). Therefore, the priest has touched your ears, that your ears may be opened to the sermon and exhortation of the priest.

CHAPTER 2

4. We have come to the font; you have entered; you have been anointed. Consider whom you have seen, what you have said; consider; repeat carefully. A Levite meets you; a priest meets you; you are anointed as an athlete of Christ, as if to contend in the contest of this world. You have professed the struggles of your contest. He who contends has what he hopes for; where there is a struggle, there is a crown. You contend in the world, but you are crowned by Christ. And for the struggles of the world you are crowned, for, although the reward is in heaven, the merit for the reward is established here.

5. When you were asked: "Do you renounce the devil and his works?"—what did you reply? "I do renounce." "Do you renounce the world and its pleasures?"—what did you reply? "I do renounce." Be mindful of your words, and never let the sequence of your bond be broken. If you give a man surety, you are held responsible, so that you may receive his money; you are held bound, and the lender binds you if you resist. If you refuse, you go to a judge and there you will be convicted by your own bond.

6. Consider where you promised, or to whom you promised. You saw the Levite, but he is the minister of Christ. You saw him minister before the altar. Therefore, your surety is held, not on earth, but in heaven. Consider where you receive the heavenly sacraments. If the body of Christ is here, here, too, are the angels established. "Wheresoever the body shall be, there shall the eagles also be" (Mt 24.28), you have read in the Gospel. Wheresoever the body shall be, there shall the eagles also be, who are accustomed to fly so as to escape the earthly and to seek the heavenly. Why do I

say this? Because men, too, are angels, whoever announce Christ and seem to be received into the place of angels.

7.   How? Observe John the Baptist was born of a man and a woman. Yet give heed, because he himself also is an Angel. "Behold, I send my angel before your face, who shall prepare your way before you" (Mal 3.1; Mt 11.10). Observe again. Malachi the Prophet says: "For the lips of the priest shall keep knowledge and they shall seek the law at his mouth: because he is the angel of the Lord of hosts" (Mal 2.7). These words are spoken for this reason, that we may proclaim the glory of the priesthood, not that something may be arrogated to personal merits.

8.   So you have renounced the universe; you have renounced the world; be solicitous. He who owes money always considers his bond. And you who owe Christ faith keep faith, which is much more precious than money; for faith is an eternal patrimony, money a temporal one. And do you, therefore, always remember what you have promised; you will be more cautious. If you keep your promise, you will also keep your bond.

CHAPTER 3

9.   Then you approached nearer; you saw the font; you also saw the priest above the font. I cannot doubt that could not have fallen upon your mind, which fell upon that Syrian Naaman, for, although he was cleansed, yet he doubted first. Why? I shall tell you; observe:

10.   You entered; you saw water; you saw the priest; you saw the Levite. Lest, perchance, someone say: "Is this all?"—yes, this is all, truly all, where there is all innocence, where there is all piety, all grace, all sanctification. You have seen what you were able to see with the eyes of your body, with human perception; you have not seen those things which are effected but those which are seen. Those which are not seen are much greater than those which are seen, for the things which are seen are temporal, but the things which are not seen are eternal.

CHAPTER 4

11. Therefore, let us say first—Hold the bond of my words and exact it—"We marvel at the mysteries of the Jews which were handed down to our fathers, first the age of the sacraments, then the sanctity of those who vouch for them." This I assure you, that the sacraments of the Christians are more divine and earlier than those of the Jews.

12. What superiority is there over the people of the Jews having passed through the sea, that meanwhile we may speak of baptism? Yet the Jews who passed through, all died in the desert. But he who passes through this font, that is from the earthly to the heavenly—for there is a passage here, thus Easter, that is, "His passage," the passage from sin to life, from fault to grace, from defilement to sanctification—he who passes through this font does not die but rises.

CHAPTER 5

13. Naaman then was leprous. A girl said to his wife: "If my master wishes to be made clean, let him go to the land of Israel, and there he will find him who can rid him of leprosy." She told her mistress, and the wife told her husband, Naaman the king of Syria, who sent him, as one most acceptable to himself, to the king of Israel. The king of Israel heard that he had been sent to him to be cleansed of leprosy, and rent his garment. Then Elisha the Prophet commands him: "Why is it that you have rent your garment, as if there were no powerful God to cleanse the leper? Send him to me." He sent him. When he approaches, the prophet says "Come, go down to the Jordan, dip and be cured."

14. He began to ponder with himself and say: "Is this all? I have come from Syria to the land of Judea and I am told: 'Come to the Jordan and dip and you will be cured,' as if the rivers in my own country were not better." His servants said to him: "Lord, why do you not do the word of the prophet? Rather, do it and try." Then he went to the Jordan, dipped and arose cured (2 Kgs 5. 1–14).

15. What, then, does this mean? You have seen water: not all water cures, but the water which has the grace of Christ cures. One is an element, the other a consecration; one an opus, the other an operation. Opus belongs to water; operation belongs to the Holy Spirit. Water does not cure unless the Holy Spirit descends and consecrates that water, as you have read that, when our Lord Jesus gave the form of baptism, He came to John, and John said to Him: "I ought to be baptized by you; and you come to me?" Christ replied to him: "Suffer it now: for so it becomes us to fulfill all justice" (Mt 3.14, 15). Behold that all justice is established in baptism.

16. Therefore, why did Christ descend, except that flesh of yours might be cleansed, the flesh which he took over from our condition? For no washing away of His sins was necessary for Christ, "who did no sin" (1 Pet 2.22), but it was necessary for us who remain subject to sin. Therefore, if baptism is for our sakes, the form has been established for us, faith has been set forth.

17. Christ descended; John stood by, who baptized, and behold! The Holy Spirit descended as a dove. Not a dove descended, but "as a dove." Remember what I said: "Christ took on flesh, not 'as flesh,' but that true flesh of yours; Christ truly took on flesh. But the Holy Spirit in the likeness of a dove, not as a real dove, but in the likeness of a dove descended from heaven." So John saw and believed.

18. Christ descended; the Holy Spirit also descended. Why did Christ descend first, the Holy Spirit afterward, when the form and practice of baptism includes this: that the font be consecrated first, then that he descend who is to be baptized. For, when the priest first enters, he performs the exorcism according to the creation of water; afterward he delivers an invocation and prayer, that the font may be sanctified and that the presence of the eternal Trinity may be at hand. But Christ descended first, and the Spirit followed. For what reason? Not that the Lord Jesus himself might seem to be in need of the mystery of sanctification, but that himself might sanctify, that the Spirit also might sanctify.

19. So Christ descended into the water, and the Holy Spirit descended as a dove; God the Father also spoke from heaven: You have the mystery of the Trinity.

CHAPTER 6

20. Moreover, the Apostle says that in the Red Sea there was a figure of this baptism, in these words: "All our fathers were baptized in the cloud and in the sea," and he added: "Now all these things happened to them in figure" (1 Cor 10.11), but to us in reality. Then Moses held the staff. The people of the Jews were shut in. The Egyptian approached with armed men. On one side the Hebrews were shut in by the sea. They were unable to cross the sea or to turn back against the enemy. They began to murmur.

21. Behold, let it not provoke you that they were heard. Although the Lord heard, yet they are not without fault who murmured. It is your duty, when you are restrained, to believe that you will go forth, not to murmur: to invoke, to question, not to express a complaint.

22. Moses held a staff and led the people of the Hebrews by night in a pillar of light, by day in a pillar of cloud. What is light but truth, since it gives forth an open and clear brightness? What is a column of light but the Lord Christ, who has dispelled the shadows of infidelity, has infused the light of truth and grace into human inclinations? But surely the column of a cloud is the Holy Spirit. The people were in the sea and the column of light went ahead, then the column of a cloud followed like the shadow of the Holy Spirit. You see that by the Holy Spirit and by the water he displayed a figure of baptism.

23. In the flood, also, already at that time there was a figure of baptism, and still, of course, there were no mysteries among the Jews. If, then, the form of this baptism preceded, you see that the mysteries of the Christians are older than were those of the Jews.

24. But, meanwhile, in consideration of the weakness of my voice and reasons of time, let it suffice today to have tasted the mysteries even from the sacred font. On tomorrow, if the Lord grants the power of speaking or the opportunity, I shall go into the matter more fully. There is need of your sanctity having ears prepared and minds more ready so as to be able to grasp what we can gather from the series of the Scriptures and shall go into, that you may have the grace of the Father and of the Son and of the Holy Spirit, to which Trinity is the everlasting kingdom from the ages and now and always, and forever and ever. Amen.

THE SACRAMENTS: II

14. Now, then, let us take thought. A priest comes; he says a prayer at the font; he invokes the name of the Father, the presence of the Son and of the Holy Spirit; he uses heavenly words. The words are heavenly, because they are Christ's, that we baptize: "In the Name of the Father and of the Son and of the Holy Spirit" (Mt 28.19). If, then, at the words of men, at the invocation of a holy man, the Trinity was present, how much more is the Trinity present there where eternal words operate? Do you wish to know that the Spirit came down? You have heard that He came down as a dove. Why as a dove? That the unbelievers might be called to faith. In the beginning there ought to have been a sign; in later generations there ought to be perfection.

16. Now let us examine what it is that is called baptism! You came to the font; you went down into it; you gave heed to the highest priest; you saw the Levites (deacons) and the priest at the font. What is baptism?

17. In the beginning our Lord God made man so that, if he had not tasted sin, he would not have died the death. He contracted sin; he was made subject to death; he was ejected from paradise. But the Lord, who wished his benefits to endure and to abolish all the snares of the serpent, also to abolish everything that caused harm, first, however, passed sentence on man: "Dust you are and into dust you shall return" (Gen 2.7), and He made man subject to death. It was a divine sentence; it could not be resolved by a human condition. A remedy was given: that man should die and rise again. Why? That also, which he had before ceded to a place of damnation, might cede to a place of benefit. What is this except death? Do you ask how? Because death intervening makes an end to sin. For when we die, surely we have ceased to sin. The satisfaction of the sentence seemed to be that man, who had been made to live, if he had not sinned, began to die. But that the perpetual grace of God might persevere, man died, but Christ found resurrection, that is, to restore the heavenly benefit which had been lost by the deceit of the serpent. Both, then, are for our good, for death is the end of sins and resurrection is the reformation of nature.

18. However, lest in this world the deceit and snares of the evil might prevail, baptism was found. Hear what Scripture—rather, the Son of God—says about this baptism, that the Pharisees, who did not wish to be baptized by John's baptism, "despised the counsel of God" (Lk 7.30). Then baptism is the counsel of God. How great is grace, where there is the counsel of God!

19. Listen then: For that in this world, also, the grip of the Devil might be loosened, there was discovered how man alive might die and alive might rise again. What is "alive"? That is: the living life of the body, when it came to the font, and dipped into the font. What is water but of earth? So it satisfied the heavenly sentence without the stupor of death. Because you dip, that sentence is resolved: "You are dust and into dust you shall return." When the sentence has been fulfilled, there is opportunity for heavenly benefit and remedy. So water is of earth, but the potentials of our life did not permit that we be covered with earth and rise again from earth. Then earth does not wash, but water washes. Therefore, the font is as a sepulchre.

CHAPTER 7

20. You were asked: "Do you believe in God the Father almighty?" You said: "I do believe," and you dipped, that is: you were buried. Again you were asked: "Do you believe in our Lord Jesus Christ and in his cross?" You said: "I do believe," and you dipped. So you were also buried together with Christ. For who is buried with Christ rises again with Christ. A third time you were asked: "Do you believe also in the Holy Spirit?" You said: "I do believe," you dipped a third time, so that the threefold confession absolved the multiple lapse of the higher life.

21. Finally, to furnish you an example, the holy Apostle Peter, after he seemed to have lapsed by the weakness of his human condition, who had before denied, afterward, that he might wipe out and resolve the lapse, is asked a third time, if he loved Christ. Then he said: "You know that I love you" (Jn 21.18). He said it a third time that he might be absolved a third time.

22. Thus, then, the Father dismisses sin; thus the Son dismisses it; thus, too, the Holy Spirit. But do not marvel that we are baptized in one name, that is, "In the Name of the Father, and of the Son, and of the Holy Spirit," because He said one name, in which is one substance, one divinity, one majesty. This is the name of which it is said: "Whereby we must be saved" (Acts 4.12). In this name you all have been saved; you have returned to the grace of life.

23. So the Apostle exclaims, as you heard in the reading of the Gospel today, that whoever is baptized is baptized into the death of Jesus. What is in the death? That just as Christ died to sin and lives unto God, so you, too, died to the former allurements of sins through the sacrament of baptism and rose again through the grace of Christ. So death is, but not in the reality of corporal death but in likeness. For when you dip, you take on the likeness of death and burial, you received the sacrament of that cross, because Christ hung on the cross and His body was transfixed with nails. You then are crucified with Him; you cling to Christ, you cling to the nails of our Lord Jesus Christ, lest the Devil be able to take you from Him. Let the nail of Christ hold you, whom the weakness of human condition recalls.

24. So you dipped; you came to the priest. What did he say to you? He said: "God the Father Almighty, who regenerated you by water and the Holy Spirit and forgave you your sins, Himself will anoint you unto life everlasting." See, unto what you were anointed, he said: "Unto life everlasting." Do not prefer this life to that life. For example, if some enemy rises up, if he wishes to take away your faith, if he threatens death, that someone may prevaricate, beware what you choose. Do not choose that in which you are not anointed, but choose that in which you are anointed, so that you prefer eternal life to temporal life.

SACRAMENTS: III

CHAPTER 1

1. Yesterday we discussed the font, whose likeness is as a kind of sepulchre into which, believing in the Father and the Son and the Holy Spirit, we are received and dipped and rise, that is, are resuscitated. Moreover, you receive chrism, that is, ointment upon the head. Why upon the head? Because, "The eyes of a wise man are in his head" (Eccl 2.14). Solomon says. For wisdom without grace grows cold, but when wisdom has received grace, then its work begins to be perfect. This is called regeneration.

2. What is regeneration? You have it in the Acts of the Apostles, from that line which is mentioned in the second psalm, "You are my Son, this day have I begotten you" (Ps 2.7), seems to refer to the resurrection. For the holy Apostle Peter in the Acts of the Apostles thus interpreted, that at that time, when the Son rose from the dead, the voice of the Father resounded: "You are my Son, this day I have begotten you." Therefore, He is also called the first born from the dead." So, what is resurrection other than we rise from death unto life? Thus, then, even in baptism, since it is a likeness of death, undoubtedly, when you dip and rise again, it becomes a likeness of resurrection. Thus, according to the interpretation of the Apostle, just as that resurrection was a regeneration, so that resurrection from the font is a regeneration.

3. But why do you say that you dip in water? For this reason do you roam about; for this reason does uncertainty hold you? Indeed, we read: "Let the earth bring forth fruit from itself, and the earth brings forth yielding fruit." Similarly, too, you have read about water: "Let the waters bring forth creatures having life" (Gen 1.20), and creatures having life were born. They indeed were in the beginning of creation, but for you it was reserved for water to regenerate you unto grace, just as water generated other creatures unto life. Imitate the fish, which indeed has obtained less grace, yet should be an object of wonder to you. It is in the sea and swims upon the floods. A tempest rages in the sea, storms shriek, but the fish swims; it is not submerged because it is accustomed to swim. So even for you this world is a sea. It has diverse floods, heavy

waters, severe storms. And do you be a fish, that the water of the world may not submerge you. Moreover, beautifully does the Father say to the Son: "This day I have begotten you" (Ps 2.7). That is: "When you redeemed the people, when you called them to the kingdom of heaven, when you fulfilled my will, you proved that you were my son."

4. You came up from the font. What followed? You heard the reading. The girded priest—for although the presbyters also do this, the highest priest, girded, I say, washed your feet. What mystery is this? Surely, you have heard that the Lord, after He had washed the feet of the other disciples, went to Peter and Peter said to him "Do you wash my feet?" (Jn 13,6). That is, "Do you, Lord, wash the feet of a servant; do you without stain wash my feet; do you, the author of the heavens, wash my feet?" You have this also elsewhere (Mt 3.14); He went to John and John said to Him: "I ought to be baptized by you, and you come to me?" I am a sinner, and have you come to a sinner, that you who have not sinned may put aside your sins? Behold all justice, behold humility, behold grace, behold sanctification. He said: If I wash not your feet, you shalt have no part with me" (Jn 13.8).

5. We are not unaware of the fact that the Church in Rome does not have this custom, whose character and form we follow in all things. Yet it does not have the custom of washing the feet. So note: perhaps on account of the multitude this practice declined. Yet there are some who say and try to allege in excuse that this is not to be done in the mystery, nor in baptism, nor in regeneration, but the feet are to be washed as for a guest. But one belongs to humility, the other to sanctification. Finally, be aware that the mystery is also sanctification: "If I wash not your feet, you shalt have no part with me." So I say this, not that I may rebuke others, but that I may commend my own ceremonies. In all things I desire to follow the Church in Rome, yet we, too, have human feeling; what is preserved more rightly elsewhere we, too, preserve more rightly.

6. We follow the Apostle Peter himself: we cling to his devotion. What does the Church in Rome reply to this? Surely for us the very author of this assertion is the Apostle Peter, who was the

priest of the Church in Rome, Peter himself, when he said: "Lord, not only my feet, but also my hands and my head" (Jn 13:9). Behold faith: That he first pleaded an excuse belonged to humility; that he afterward offered himself belonged to devotion and faith.

7. The Lord answered him, because he had said "hands and head": "He that is washed, needs not to wash again but to wash his feet alone" (Jn 13.9). So fault withdraws. But since Adam was overthrown by the Devil and venom was poured out upon his feet, accordingly you wash the feet, that in this part, in which the serpent lay in wait, greater aid of sanctification may be added, that afterward he cannot overthrow you. Therefore, you wash the feet, that you may wash away the poisons of the serpent. It is also of benefit for humility, that we may not be ashamed in the mystery of what we disdain in obedience.

CHAPTER 2

8. There follows a spiritual sign which you hear read today, because after the font there remains the effecting of perfection, when at the invocation of the priest the Holy Spirit is poured forth, "the spirit of wisdom, and of understanding, the spirit of counsel, and of virtue, the spirit of knowledge, and of godliness, the spirit of holy fear" (Is 11.2, 3), as it were, seven virtues of the Spirit.

9. All virtues, of course, pertain to the Spirit, but these are, as it were, cardinal: as it were, principal. For what is so principal as godliness? What is so principal as knowledge of God? What is so principal as fear of God? Just as fear of this world is infirmity, so fear of God is great fortitude.

10. There are seven virtues, when you are signed. For as the Holy Apostle says, because the wisdom of our Lord is manifold, he says, and the wisdom of God is manifold, so is the Holy Spirit manifold, who has diverse and various virtues. Therefore, He is called the "God of hosts," which can be applied to the Father and the Son and the Holy Spirit. But this belongs to another discussion, to another time.

11. After this what follows? You are able to come to the altar. Since you have come, you are able to see what you did not see before. This is a mystery that you have read in the Gospel; if, however, you have not read it—certainly you have heard it: A blind man presents himself to the Savior to be cured, and He who cured others only by a word and speech and by His power restored the sight of eyes, yet in the book of the Gospel which is written according to John, who truly before the rest saw great mysteries and pointed them out and declared them, wished to prefigure this mystery in him. Surely, all the Evangelists were holy, all the Apostles; all were holy except the betrayer. Yet St. John who was the last to write his Gospel, as if a friend required and chosen by Christ, poured forth the eternal mysteries by a kind of greater trumpet. Whatever he has said is a mystery. Another said that the blind man was cured. Matthew said it. What does John alone say? —"He took clay and spread it upon his eyes and said to him: 'Go to Siloe.' And rising he went and washed and he came seeing" (Jn 9.7).

12. Do you also consider the eyes of your heart? You saw the things that are corporeal with corporeal eyes, but the things that are of the sacraments you were not yet able to see with the eyes of the heart. So, when you gave your name, he took mud and besmeared it over your eyes. What does this signify? That you confessed your sin, that you examined your conscience, that you performed penance for your sins, that is, that you recognize the lot of human generation. For, even if he who comes to baptism does not confess sin, nevertheless by this very fact he fulfills the confession of all sins, in that he seeks to be baptized so as to be justified, that is so as to pass from fault to grace.

13. Do not think it a matter of indifference. There are some—I know for certain that there was someone who said it—when we said to him: "In this age you ought rather to be baptized," he said: "Why am I baptized? I have no sin; I have not contracted sin, have I?" This one did not have the mud, because Christ had not besmeared him, that is, He had not opened his eyes; for no man is without sin.

14. He who takes refuge in the baptism of Christ recognizes himself as human. So, too, He placed mud upon you, that is, modesty, prudence, consideration of your frailty, and said to you: "Go to Siloe" "Which," he says, "is interpreted sent," That is: Go to that font, at which the cross of Christ the Lord is preached; go to that font, at which Christ redeemed the errors of all.

15. You went, you washed, you came to the altar, you began to see what you had not seen before. That is: Through the font of the Lord and the preaching of the Lord's passion, your eyes were then opened. You who seemed before to have been blind in heart began to see the light of the sacraments.

So, most beloved brethren, we have come all the way to the altar, to the richer discussion. And thus, since this is a matter of time, we cannot begin the whole disputation, since the discussion is more comprehensive. What has been said today is enough. Tomorrow, if it please the Lord, we will discuss the sacraments themselves.

THE SACRAMENTS: IV

CHAPTER 1

1. In the Old Testament the priests were accustomed to enter the first tabernacle frequently; the highest priest entered the second tabernacle once a year. Evidently recalling this to the Hebrews, the Apostle Paul explains the series of the Old Testament. For there was manna in the second tabernacle; there was also the rod of Aaron, that had withered and afterward blossomed, and the censer (Num 17.2–10).

2. To what does this point? That you may understand what the second tabernacle is, in which the priest introduced you , in which once a year the highest priest is accustomed to enter, that is, the baptistery, where the rod of Aaron flourished. Formerly it was dry; afterward it blossomed: And you were dried, and you begin to flower by the watering of the font. You had become dry by sins, you had become dry by errors and transgressions, but now you began to bring forth fruit "planted near the running waters" (Ps 1.3).

CHAPTER 2

5. There follows your coming to the altar. You began to come; the angels observed; they saw you approaching, and that human condition which before was stained with the shadowy squalor of sins they saw suddenly shining bright, and so they said: "Who is this that cometh up from the desert whitewashed?" So the angels also marvel. Do you wish to know how they marvel? Hear the Apostle Peter saying that those things have been conferred on you which the angels also desired to see. Hear again. It says: "The eye has not seen nor the ear heard what things God has prepared for them that love him" (1 Cor 2.9).

6. Then recognize what you have received. The holy Prophet David saw this grace in figure and desired it. Do you wish to know how he desired it? Again hear him as he says: "You shalt sprinkle me with hyssop, and I shall be cleansed; you shalt wash me and I shall be made whiter than snow" (Ps 51.7). Why? Because snow, although it is white, quickly grows dark with some filth and is corrupted; that grace which you have received, if you hold fast what you have received, will be lasting and perpetual.

7. You came, then, desiring; inasmuch as you had seen so much grace, you came to the altar desiring to receive the sacrament. Your soul says: "And I will go in to the altar of God, to God who gives joy to my youth" (Ps 43.4). You laid aside the old age of sins, you took on the youth of grace. The heavenly sacraments have bestowed this upon you. Finally, again, hear David as he says: "Your youth will be renewed like the eagle's" (Ps 103.5). You have begun to be a good eagle which seeks heaven, disdains earthly things. Good eagles are about the altar, for "Wheresoever the body shall be, there shall the eagles also be gathered together" (Lk 17:37). The form of the body is the altar, and the body of Christ is on the altar, you are the eagles renewed by the washing away of transgression.

CHAPTER 4

13. Therefore, who is the author of the sacraments but the Lord Jesus? Those sacraments came down from heaven, for all counsel is from heaven. Moreover, truly, a great and divine miracle, that

God rained manna from heaven upon the people, and the people did not labor and did eat.

14. You perhaps say: "My bread is usual." But that bread is bread before the words of the sacraments; when consecration has been added, from bread it becomes the flesh of Christ. So let us confirm this, how it is possible that what is bread is the body of Christ. By what words, then, is the consecration and by whose expressions? By those of the Lord Jesus. For all the rest that are said in the preceding are said by the priest: praise to God, prayer is offered, there is petition for the people, for kings, for the rest. When it comes to performing a venerable sacrament, then the priest uses not his own expressions, but he uses the expressions of Christ. Thus the expression of Christ performs this sacrament.

15. What is the expression of Christ? Surely that by which all things were made. The Lord ordered, the heaven was made; the Lord ordered, the earth was made; the Lord ordered, the seas were made; the Lord ordered, every creature was generated. You see then how the creating expression of the Lord Jesus, that those things might begin to be which were not, how much more creating, that those things be which were, and be changed to something else. The heaven was not, the sea was not, the earth was not, but hear David as he says: "He spoke, and they were made; He commanded and they were created" (Ps 148.5).

16. Therefore, to reply to you, there was no body of Christ before consecration, but after the consecration I say to you that now there is the body of Christ. He Himself spoke and it was made: He Himself commanded and it was created. You yourself were, but you were an old creature; after you were consecrated, you began to be a new creature. Do you wish to know how a new creature? It says: "Every creature is new in Christ" (2 Cor 5.1)

CHAPTER 5

21. Do you wish to know how it is consecrated with heavenly words? Accept what the words are. The priest speaks. He says: "Perform for us this oblation written, reasonable, acceptable, which is a figure of the body and blood of our Lord Jesus Christ.

On the day before He suffered He took bread in His holy hands looked toward heaven, toward you, holy Father omnipotent, eternal God, giving thanks, blessed, broke, and having broken it gave it to the Apostles and His disciples, saying: "Take and eat of this, all of you; for this is my body, which shall be broken for many." Take note.

22. "Similarly also, on the day before He suffered, after they had dined, He took the chalice, looked toward heaven, toward thee, holy Father omnipotent, eternal God and giving thanks He blessed it, and gave it to the Apostles and His disciples, saying: "Take and drink of this, all of you, for this is my blood." Behold! All these words up to "Take" are the Evangelist's, whether body or blood. From then on the words are Christ's: "Take and drink of this all of you; for this is my blood."

23. Look at these events one by one. It says: "On the day before He suffered, He took bread in his holy hands." Before it is consecrated, it is bread; but when Christ's words have been added, it is the body of Christ. Finally, hear him as He says: "Take and eat of this, all of you; for this is my body." And before the words of Christ, the chalice is full of wine and water; when the words of Christ have been added, then blood is effected, which redeemed the people. So behold in what great respects the expression of Christ is able to change all things. Then the Lord Jesus Himself testified to us that we receive his body and blood. Should we doubt at all about his faith and testification?

24. Now return with me to my proposition. Great and venerable indeed is the fact that manna rained upon the Jews from heaven. But understand! What is greater, manna from heaven or the body of Christ? Surely the body of Christ, who is the Author of heaven. Then, he who ate the manna died; he who has eaten this body will effect for himself remission of sins and "shall not die forever" (Jn 6.51).

25. So you say not indifferently "Amen," already confessing in spirit that you receive the body of Christ. Therefore, when you ask, the priest says to you: "the body of Christ," and you say: "Amen," that is, "Truly." What the tongue confesses let the

affection hold. That you may know, moreover: "This is a sacrament, whose figure went on before."

CHAPTER 6

26. Next realize how great a sacrament it is. See what He says: "As often as you shall do this, so often will you do a commemoration of me, until I come again."

27. And the priest says: "Therefore, mindful of His most glorious passion and resurrection from the dead and ascension into heaven, we offer you this immaculate victim, a reasonable sacrifice, an unbloody victim, this holy bread, and chalice of eternal life. And we ask and pray that you accept this offering upon your sublime altar through the hands of your angels, just as you deigned to accept the gifts of your just son Abel and the sacrifice of our patriarch Abraham and what the highest priest Melchisedec offered you."

28. So, as often as you receive, what does the Apostle say to you? "As often as we receive, we proclaim the death of the Lord" (1 Cor 11.26). If death, we proclaim the remission of sins. If, as often as blood is shed, it is shed for the remission of sins, I, who always sin, should always have a remedy.

29. Meanwhile, today also we have explained according to our ability. But tomorrow, on the seventh day and Sunday we shall speak about the order of prayer, as we are able. May our Lord God keep for you the grace which He gave, and may He deign to illuminate more fully the eyes which He gave you, through His Only-begotten Son, King and Savior, our Lord God, through whom He has, with whom he has praise, honor, glory, magnificence, power, together with the Holy Spirit, from the ages and now and always, and forever and ever. Amen.

CHAPTER FOURTEEN

THE BAPTISMAL HOMILIES OF THEODORE OF MOPSUESTIA

Theodore, a fellow student of John Chrysostom in the school of the pagan rehetorician Libanius at Antioch, was ordained priest in Antioch in 383. Under the influence of Chrysostom he entered the monastic life. After a brief lapse, and once again at the urging of Chrysostom, he returned to the monastery. He remained in Antioch until he became bishop of Mopsuestia in Cilicia in 393. He died in Mopsuestia in 428. The Baptismal Homilies which appear below were preached at Antioch, probably about the year 390. Antioch as well as Alexandria were major centers of Christianity in the closing decades of the fourth century. They adopted different approaches to the interpretation of scripture, Antioch favoring a more literal interpretation while Alexandria favored a more allegorical interpretation. More importantly, they differed in their explanation of the mystery of the unity of two natures, human and divine, in the one person of Jesus. Both explanations attempted to preserve the essential unity of the person of Jesus. The explanation offered by the theologians of Alexandria stressed the divinity of Jesus, but in such a way that they appeared to compromise the complete humanity of Jesus. The explanation of the theologians of Antioch stressed the humanity of Jesus in such a way that they appeared to compromise the complete divinity of Jesus. As a theologian of Antioch, Theodore gives expression to this emphasis when he speaks of the Word "assuming a man" (Baptismal Homily, 3.21, 24; 5.2, 10) rather than of the "Word becoming flesh." The Antiochene tendency led to the error of Nestorius, who taught that Jesus was two persons, human and divine, united in no more than a functional or moral unity. Theodore died on the eve of the Nestorian controversy. Although he was condemned in 553 at the Council of Constantinople and most of his writings destroyed, his orthodoxy was not questioned during his lifetime. Despite his condemnation, some very able historical theologians defend his orthodoxy. His surviving writings include a

Syriac version of his sixteen **Cathechetical Lectures.** *The first eleven of these are instructions to cathechumens preparing for baptism; the last five instruct them in the meaning of the sacraments of initiation. Despite his rhetorical flourishes, Theodore writes with admirable clarity, and while a modern reader will not be sympathetic to his strained attempt to establish a correspondence between the ceremonies of the Liturgy and incidents in Christ's passion (a tendency which later commentators continued well into this century), there are other elements in Theodore's teaching about the sacraments, such as his emphasis on the central role of the Holy Spirit, the redemptive significance of Christ's resurrection, and the Liturgy as the offering of the entire community, which we can appreciate today. These insights unfortunately were lost sight of in later generations and have been recovered only in recent decades. Of the last five* **Baptismal Homilies,** *the first treats of preliminaries and is not presented here. Of the last four, II and III treat of Baptism, while IV and V treat of the Eucharist. It will be noted that Theodore places the anointing of the candidate with the Holy Spirit after Baptism, whereas his contemporary in Antioch, John Chrysostom, and the Syriac liturgical tradition which he inherited, places the anointing before baptism. Different practices in the same city at the same time are difficult, perhaps impossible, to reconcile. The translation here has been compressed. A * represents a sentence which the translator has compressed; a series of dots represent omissions either by the translator or present editor. Two sections of Homily V (30–32) which repeat what has gone before and then of the moral dispositions of the communicant have been omitted by the translator, and most of the final sections (33–43) which treat of Penance, have been omitted by this editor.*
[Translation: Yarnold, pp. 176–256]

BAPTISMAL HOMILY—II

1. I have already instructed you sufficiently about the rites which according to ancient tradition the candidates for baptism must celebrate. When you present yourselves to give in your names, in the hope of finding a dwelling place in heaven, the exorcisms are, so to say, a law-suit with the devil; you are freed from slavery to him by God's judgment. So you recite the words of the Creed and the Lord's Prayer; and there and then through the mediation of the

bishops you make an understanding to persevere in love toward God's being . . . But you need to learn what takes place in the mystery itself. . . .

2. *You stand again on sackcloth, bare-footed, with your outer garment removed and your hands stretched out to God in the attitude of prayer.*

3. *First you fall on your knees, but keep the rest of your body upright.* You stretch out your hands in the attitude of prayer. For we have fallen into sin and the sentence of death has thrown us to the ground; . . . you must kneel as a sign of your ancient fall and adore God, the source of good.

4. *The rest of your body should remain upright,* looking up to heaven. By this attitude you present, so to speak, a request to God, asking him like a petitioner for liberation from your ancient fall and a share in the joys of heaven. While you are kneeling like this the appointed ministers come and address to you in effect the very words which the angel who appeared to St Cornelius spoke to him (cf. Acts 10.4): "Your prayer has been heard." . . .

5. "I renounce Satan and all his angels, all his service, all his vanity and all his worldly enticements. I pledge myself by vow, I believe, I am baptized in the name of the Father, of the Son and of the Holy Spirit." Now the deacons come to you and tell you to recite these words. . . .

6. . . . By this you mean: Now we have nothing in common with him. . . . Once for all I renounce Satan, I avoid his company and pledge myself by vow never to seek it again. I shall have nothing to do with him, I shall avoid him like a dangerous enemy, for he was the cause of evils without number . . . This is the meaning of "I renounce."

7. . . . invisible though he [Satan] is, he can attack us with visible weapons, by means of men whom he has conquered and made instruments of his malice to harm others. That is why you add, "And all his angels."

8. His angels are men who have contracted from him some ill-will which leads them to harm others. . . . We must take "angels of Sa-

tan" to refer to all those who devote themselves to profane wisdom and spread the error of paganism. . . .

9. . . . "Angels of Satan" are the leaders and teachers of error in any heresy, honored though they may be with the name of bishop or priest. . . . You have presented yourself to Christ; you have been enrolled in God's Church; being born in baptism you look forward to becoming the body and member of Christ our Lord; you will share with him and be attached to him your Head, and keep a part from all those who dare to abandon the Church's creed.

10. . . . you continue, "and all his service.'" It is not only men who are in the Evil One's service; you must also recoil in horror from the open blasphemies done in the name of religion. All pagan practices are works of Satan . . . The pursuit of astrology is clearly the service of Satan . . . Ritual washings and purifications, amulets, the practice of hanging up fermenting dough, the inspection of the bodies of animals or the movement and cries of birds . . . The worship found among heretics in the name of religion is service of Satan. . . .

11. Then you say: "And all his vanity." Satan's vanity is a plain description of everything pagans do in the name of religion. . . .

12. Next you say: "And all his worldly enticements." What do you mean by "worldly enticements"? The theater, the circus, the stadium, athletics, songs, organ-playing, dances—seeds which the devil sows in the world in the guise of amusement to lead men's souls to ruin. . . .

THE CONTRACT WITH CHRIST

13. When you say, "I renounce," you reject Satan without reserve and show that you will never turn back or take pleasure again in his company; so too, when you say, "I pledge myself by vow," you show that you will stand firm and unshakable at God's side, that you will never on any account abandon him, and that for the rest of your life you will value more than anything else the privilege of living in company with him and in accordance with his laws.*

14. But you must also add, "I believe," for as St Paul said, "whoever would draw near to God must believe that he exists" (Heb 11.6). Since God is invisible by nature, to face him and promise to persevere as members of his household you need faith. . . . That is why the words, "I believe," are followed by the words, "I am baptized." For it is with faith in what is to take place that you came forward to receive the holy gift of baptism; you mean to be reborn, to die with Christ and rise again with him, in order that this second birth may replace your first and obtain for you a share in heaven. As long as you are by nature mortal, you cannot reach your home in heaven; but when you discard this mortality in baptism and rise again with Christ and receive the sign of this new birth you hope for, you are revealed as a citizen of heaven and become a fellow-heir to the heavenly kingdom.

15. To the foregoing words you add: "In the name of the Father and of the Son and of the Holy Spirit." For such is God's nature. It is the substance which exists from all eternity, the cause of all, which created us in the beginning and now is renewing us; it is Father, Son and Holy Spirit. We approach this nature now and offer it our vows, as is just, because it has been and remains the cause of the countless great blessings we have received. We make to it our vows and promise in the future to believe in it; we invoke it when we are baptized; we hope to receive from it the blessings which are given to us now in symbol and in anticipation, and to enjoy them for ever when we rise in reality from the dead and share in the inheritance of our home in heaven.

16. You pronounce these vows and this covenant in the attitude I have described, *kneeling on the ground*, as a sign that you are paying God a debt of adoration and that you are recalling your ancient fall to earth. *But the rest of your body is upright, and you look up to heaven and stretch out your hands in the attitude of prayer.*

FIRST ANOINTING

17. When you have pronounced these vows and this covenant, the bishop comes over to you . . . *Then he signs your forehead with the oil of anointing saying: "N. is signed in the name of the Father and of the Son and of the Holy Spirit."* This is the first installment of the sacrament he is administering to you . . . The seal that you receive at this point marks you out for ever as the sheep of Christ, the soldier of the King of Heaven. As soon as a sheep is bought, it is given a mark to identify its owner; it feeds in the same pasture and lives in the same fold as the other sheep that bear the same owner's mark. And when a solider is chosen for his height and build to serve the empire, he is at once given a tattoo on his hand to show the name of the emperor in whose service he has enlisted. You have been chosen for the kingdom of heaven; you too can be identified as a soldier of the King of heaven.

18. First you receive a sign on your forehead. This is the highest and noblest part of the body . . . So you receive this mark on the forehead to show what a great privilege you are receiving. . . .

19. When the bishop has completed this ceremony of sealing your forehead, he pronounces the words I have mentioned to show that he has set you apart for the future and appointed you a soldier of the true king and a citizen of heaven. The seal shows that all this belongs to you. Immediately *your sponsor stands behind you, spreads a linen stole over your head and raises you to your feet.* You get up off your knees to show that you have abandoned your ancient fall, and have nothing to do with the earth and earthly affairs . . . To begin with, you stand naked, like prisoners and slaves; but when you receive the sign, you spread the linen cloth over your head to symbolize the freedom to which you are called, for this is the decoration that free men wear both indoors and out.

20. Now that you carry the identification-mark of a soldier of Christ our Lord, you may receive the rest of the sacraments and so acquire the full armor of the Spirit and your share in the heavenly blessings. How this happens I shall explain in detail later. What I have said is sufficient for today. So let us end our instruction in the usual way, offering praise to God the Father, to his Only-Begotten Son and to the Holy Spirit, now and for ever. Amen.

BAPTISMAL HOMILY—III

2. . . . Today I must explain the next ceremonies, for at this stage you have to come forward for baptism itself. Baptism contains the signs of the new birth which will be manifested in reality when you rise from the dead and recover all that death has stolen from you . . . You will gain this new birth by rising from the dead to a second existence, just as when you were born of a woman you entered upon the existence that death takes away from you. You will gain this in reality when the time comes for you to rise again to your new birth; but now you have faith in Christ our Lord, and while you are waiting for the resurrection you must be content with receiving symbols and signs of it in this awesome sacrament which afford you certainty of sharing in the blessings to come.

3. You come forward then for baptism, the symbol of this birth you hope for. This is why Christ our Lord calls it a second birth in his words to Nicodemus: "Unless one is born anew, he cannot see the kingdom of God" (Jn 3.3) . . . This is clearly his meaning: just as one who is born in the flesh and of the flesh is by nature subject to death, pain, corruption and all kinds of change, so we are to expect that when we are born, so to speak, of the Spirit, we shall become by nature free from all these afflictions.*

4. But Nicodemus repeated the question: "How can this be?" Jesus answered: "The wind blows where it wills and you hear the sound of it, but you do not know whence it comes or whither it goes; so it is with everyone who is born of the Spirit." He does not say a word about water; he refers to the reliability and credibility of the Spirit to establish his teaching against all doubt. For the expression "blows where it wills" indicates the Spirit's power to accomplish his will in anything. . . .

5. For the same reason St Paul says: "All of us who have been baptized into Christ Jesus were baptized into his death. We were buried therefore with him by baptism into death, so that as Christ was raised from the dead by the glory of the Father, we too might walk in newness of life" (Rom 6.3–4) . . . Believing this we come to him for baptism, because we wish now to share in his death so as to share like him in the resurrection from the dead. So when I am baptized and put my head under the water, I wish to receive the death and burial of Christ our Lord, and I solemnly profess my faith in his resurrection; when I come up out of the water, this is a sign that I believe that I am already risen.

6. These things only happen to us in symbols, but St Paul wishes to make it clear that we are not concerned with empty symbols but with realities, in which we profess our faith with longing and without hesitation. So he continues: "If we have been united with him in a death like his, we shall certainly be united with him in a resurrection like his" (Rom 6.5). He proves the present by the future, taking the splendor of what is to come as evidence of the value of these symbols, the symbols contained in baptism, the work of the Holy Spirit. You receive baptism only because you hope for the blessings to come: by dying and rising with Christ and being born to a new life, you come to share in the reality of the signs that attracted you*. . . This second birth is the work of the Holy Spirit, whom you receive in the sacrament as a kind of guarantee. So you can see what a great sacrament this is, how awesome and deserving belief in its symbolism. . . .

7. Similarly he says in another place: "It is God who establishes us with you in Christ, and has commissioned us; he has put his seal upon us and given us his Spirit in our hearts as a guarantee" (adaption of Eph 1.13–14). In another place he says: "And not only the creation, but we ourselves, who have the first-fruits of the Spirit, groan inwardly as we wait for adoption as sons, the redemption of our bodies" (Rom 8.23). We have the first fruits of the Spirit, he says, on this earth, because we receive the fullness of grace only when we enjoy the reality. "We wait for adoption as sons, the redemption of our bodies," he says, meaning that in this life we receive adoption in anticipation; we shall receive the reality when we are born again and rise from the dead, becoming at once immortal, incorruptible and free from all physical evil. . . .

SECOND ANOINTING

8. *Then you come forward to be baptized. First you strip completely.* When you have done this, *you are anointed all over with the oil of anointing in the prescribed manner*; this is a sign of immortality you will receive through baptism . . . *You are anointed all over*: unlike clothes which come into contact with part of the body, and even if they touched the whole surface of the body would still not come in contact with the internal organs, our whole nature will "put on the imperishable" (1 Cor 15.53) at the moment of the resurrection, by virtue of the working of the Holy Spirit within us.* When this anointing is conferred upon you, *the bishop begins the ceremony with the words: "N. is anointed in the name of the Father and of the Son and of the Holy Spirit,"* and the appointed ministers anoint your body all over.

BLESSING OF THE FONT

9. Next, at the time I have already explained to you, *you go down into the water that has been blessed by the bishop.* You are not baptized in ordinary water, but in the water of the second birth. Now ordinary water cannot become this other thing except by the coming of the Holy Spirit. Consequently the bishop beforehand pronounces a prescribed form of words, asking God to let the grace of the Holy Spirit come upon the water and making it capable of begetting this awesome birth, making it a womb for sacramental birth . . . the one baptized settles in the water as in a kind of womb . . . Once mortal, it becomes immortal; once corruptible, it becomes incorruptible, once changing, it becomes unchanging; by the almighty power of him who forms it.

10. A baby born of a woman has the potentiality of talking, hearing, walking and working with his hands, but is too utterly weak for any action of the kind; yet, in due time, by God's decree he becomes capable of these actions. So too one who is born by baptism possesses in himself all the potentialities of his immortal and incorruptible nature, but cannot use or exhibit them until the moment God has ordained for us to be born from the dead and attain full enjoyment of our freedom from corruption, death, pain and change. We are endowed with the potentiality for these things at baptism but gain the effective use of them only when we are no longer merely natural but spiritual, and the working of the Spirit has made the body incorruptible and the soul immutable, holding them both in his own power and preserving them . . . In this way the water becomes an awesome womb of the second birth; in this way all who go down into the water are formed again by the grace of the Holy Spirit and born again in another, higher nature. . . .

BAPTISM

11. So the water you enter is like a crucible in which you are reshaped to a higher nature: you lay aside your old mortality and assume a nature that is completely immortal and incorruptible. You are born in water because you were formed originally from earth and water, and when you fell into sin the sentence of death made you totally corruptible. . . .

12. . . . since we are by nature mortal, we need to undergo this renewal by baptism; but once we have been formed afresh by baptism and received the grace of the Holy Spirit, who will harden us more than any fire, we cannot undergo a second renewal or look to a second baptism, just as we can only hope for a single resurrection, since Christ our Lord also, as St Paul said, "being raised from the dead will never die again; death no longer has dominion over him" (Rom 6.9).

14. . . . to teach you once for all who it is who is the cause of all these blessings, . . . *the bishop stands and lays his hand on your head saying: "N. is baptized in the name of the Father and of the Son and of the Holy Spirit."* . . . This formula corresponds to our Lord's commission: "Go therefore and make disciples of all nations, baptizing them in the name of the Father and of the Son and of the Holy Spirit" (Mt 28.19). These words show that the effects are produced entirely by the Father, the Son and the Holy Spirit, who exist from all eternity, and are the cause of all things. . . .

15. This is why, when the bishop places his hand on your head, he does not say, "I baptize," but "N. is baptized"; for no man, only divine grace, is capable of making such a gift.* He goes on at once to say who it is who signs and baptizes: the words "In the name of the Father and of the Son and of the Holy Spirit" show who is responsible for the effect, and proclaim that he himself is simply the obedient minister. . . .

16. . . . the name that the bishop pronounces is not that by which the Father, the Son and the Holy Spirit are invoked individually: the name which he invokes and by which we call upon the cause of these blessings, is the divine nature existing from all eternity, the nature shared by the Father, the Son and the Holy Spirit; we call upon them in a single invocation.* We do not call upon the Father as one cause and the Son as another and the Holy Spirit as a third. The invocation is addressed to One, and toward this One we look for the enjoyment of the graces of baptism. . . .

18. Then the bishop lays his hand on your head with the words, *"In the name of the Father" and while pronouncing them pushes you down into the water.* You obediently follow the signal he gives by word and gesture, and bow down under the water. You incline your head to show your consent and to acknowledge the truth of the bishop's words that you receive the blessing of baptism from the Father. If you were free to speak at this moment you would say *"Amen"*—a word which we use as a sign of our agreement with what the bishop says . . . "Amen" is the people's response to the bishop's thanksgiving, by which they express agreement. But since at the moment of baptism you cannot speak, but have to receive the sacrament of renewal in silence and awe, you bow your head when you immerse yourself to show your sincere agreement with the bishop's words.

19. *You bow down under the water, then lift your head again. Meanwhile the bishops says, "And of the Son," and guides you with his hand as you bend down into the water as before.* You make the sign of consent as before, signifying that you accept the bishop's declaration that it is from the Son that you hope to receive the blessings of baptism. *You raise your head, and again the bishop says, "And of the Holy Spirit," pressing you down into the water with his hand.* You bend beneath the water again, humbly acknowledging by the same sign that you hope for the blessings of baptism from the Holy Spirit . . . Then you come up out of the font to receive the completion of the mystery.

20. Three times you immerse yourself, each time performing the same action, once in the name of the Father, once in the name of the Son and once in the name of the Holy Spirit. . . . This teaches you that there is only one baptism, and that the grace dispensed by the Father, the Son and the Holy Spirit is one and the same. They are inseparable one from the other, for they have one nature. So although each Person can confer the grace, as is shown by your immersion at each of the names, we do not consider baptism to be complete until the Father, the Son and the Holy Spirit have all been invoked. . . .

21. It is in this sense that St Paul says: "One Lord, one faith, one baptism, one body and one spirit, one God and Father of us all, who is through all and in all" (adapted from Eph 4.4–6) . . . what he is teaching is this: the one Lordship is the one godhead. For the substance of the Father, the Son and the Holy Spirit is one, without body or limit. It is the substance which at baptism grants us adoption, this substance in which we believe, are baptized and become a single body by the power of the Holy Spirit at baptism. This power makes us sons of God and the one body of Christ our Lord, whom we call our Head, since he shares our nature and he was the first to rise from the dead so that we might share in these blessings through him . . . In his human existence he was assumed from among us and became the first to rise from the dead, in this way assuring for us a share in his resurrection, which allows us to hope that our bodies too will be like his: "But our common wealth is in heaven, and from it we await a Savior, the Lord Jesus Christ, who will change our lowly body to be like his glorious body" (Phil 3.20–21).

22. This prediction will be fulfilled in reality at the resurrection; at baptism we merely perform the signs and symbols. For the same reason we are called, according to St Paul's saying, the body of Christ our Lord, who is our head: Christ is the head "from whom the whole body, nourished and knit together, grows with a growth that is from God" (Col 2.19).

OUR BAPTISM AND CHRIST'S BAPTISM

Our Lord himself, before his resurrection from the dead, was seen to receive baptism at the hands of John the Baptist in the River Jordan in order to present in anticipation a sign of the baptism that we were to receive by his grace. For us he was "the first-born from the dead," in St Paul's words, "that in everything he might be preeminent"; therefore he chose for your sake to be the first not only in the reality of the resurrection but also in sign.

... St John the Baptist said to him: "I need to be baptized by you, and do you come to me?" showing in this way the difference there was between himself and Jesus. But Jesus replied: "Let it be so now; for thus it is fitting for us to fulfill all righteousness" (Mt 3.14–15). Righteousness he meant, is established by the grace of baptism, and it is fitting that your hands should introduce it among those who are subject to the Law. So the Law too is publicly honored, since through it righteousness entered the world.

23. Our Lord, then, was baptized by John, but not with John's baptism. For John's baptism was a baptism of repentance for the remission of sins, and our Lord had no need of it as he was free from all sin. He was baptized with our baptism, and presented an anticipation of it. Consequently he also received the Holy Spirit, who appeared descending in the form of a dove and "remained on him" (Jn 1.32) as the evangelist says. For John did not have the power to confer the Spirit, he said himself ... The power to confer the Spirit belonged to our Lord. He gives us "the first fruits of the Spirit" (Rom 8.23) now, and promises to give us the full measure at the resurrection, when our nature will be fully capable of being transformed in reality to a state of excellence.*

24. You were baptized, then, with the same baptism that Christ our Lord received in his humanity. This is one reason why you are baptized "in the name of the Father and of the Son and of the Holy Spirit," because the very events at Christ's baptism foreshadowed your baptism in sign. When the Father said aloud from far off, "This is my beloved Son, with whom I am well pleased," he was referring in fact to the grace of our adoption, which is the purpose of baptism. ...

25. When the bishop says, "In the name of the Father," he recalls the Father's words: "This is my beloved Son, with whom I am well pleased." When he says, "Of the Son," take these words to refer to him who was present in the man who was baptized, and acknowledge that he has obtained adoption for you. When he says, "Of the Holy Spirit," remember the one who descended in the form of a dove and remained on him, and in short expect that your adoption too will be confirmed by the same Spirit. For, as St Paul said, "those who are led by the Spirit of God are sons of God." The only genuine adoption is that granted by the Holy Spirit; but it is not genuine if the Spirit is not present to produce the effect and encourage us to receive the gift in which we have faith. And so, by the invocation of the Father, the Son and the Holy Spirit, you have received the grace of adoption.

Then you come up out of the font. You have received baptism, second birth. By your immersion you fulfilled the sentence of burial; by coming up you received a sign of the resurrection. You have been born again and have become a completely different man. You no longer belong to Adam, who was subject to change, because he was afflicted and overwhelmed by sin; you belong to Christ, who was entirely free from sin through his resurrection, and in fact had committed no sin from the beginning of his life. For it was fitting that he should have from the beginning a claim to the immutable nature that he received in full at the resurrection. So it is that he confirms for us the resurrection from the dead and a share in his freedom from corruption.

THE WHITE GARMENT

26. As soon as *you come up out of the font, you put on a dazzling garment of pure white.* This is a sign of the world of shining splendor and the way of life to which you have already passed in symbol. When you experience the resurrection in reality and put on immortality and incorruptibility, you will not need such garments any longer; but you need them now, because you have not yet received these gifts in reality, but only in symbols and signs. . . .

ANOINTING WITH THE SPIRIT

27. When you have received grace by means of baptism, then, and put on this shining white garment, *the bishop comes to you and puts a seal on your forehead, saying: "N. is sealed in the name of the Father and of the Son and of the Holy Spirit."* When Jesus came up out of the water, he received the grace of the Holy Spirit, which came and remained on him in the form of a dove. This is why he too is said to have been anointed by the Holy Spirit: "The Spirit of the Lord is upon me," he said, "and therefore the Lord has anointed me."

"Jesus of Nazareth, whom God anointed with the Holy Spirit and with power." This shows that the Holy Spirit never leaves him, just as the anointing attaches to those who are anointed by men with oil and never leaves them. You too, then, must be sealed on the forehead. *While the bishop is putting the seal on you, he says: "N. is sealed in the name of the Father, etc."* This sign shows you that, when the Father, the Son and the Holy Spirit were named, the Holy Spirit came upon you. You were anointed by him and received him by God's grace. He is yours and remains within you. You enjoy the first-fruits of him in this life, for you receive now in symbol the possession of the blessings to come. Then you will receive the grace in its fullness, and it will free you from death, corruption, pain and change; your body too will last forever and will be free from decay, and your soul will not be liable to any further movement toward evil.

28. Such, then, is the second birth which we receive at baptism, and which you are now about to approach. We hope that this baptism will enable us to pass in reality to this dread birth of the resurrection. Baptism assures us of the resurrection, a resurrection which in signs and symbols we already enjoy sacramentally by faith.*. . .

29. When you have undergone the sacramental birth of baptism in this way, you will come forward to receive the food of immortality, the food that will be in keeping with your birth. On a later occasion you will be able to learn about this food and the way in which it is offered to you. But now at the end of this instruction you are going to receive the birth of baptism; you have come forward now to share in the indescribable light by means of this second birth. So for the moment our words have, so to speak, wound you tightly in swaddling bands to keep you in mind of this birth which is about to take place. Here, then, we shall let you rest in silence; at a suitable time we shall bring you to this divine food and explain it to you. But now let us end our address in the usual way, praising God the Father, his Only-begotten Son and the Holy Spirit, now and for ever. Amen.

BAPTISMAL HOMILY—IV

THE PRESENTATION OF THE OFFERINGS

25. . . . When the offering which is about to be presented is brought out in the sacred vessels, on the patens and in the chalice, you must imagine that Christ our Lord is being led out to his passion. . . . So you must regard deacons as representations of the invisible ministering powers when they carry up the bread for the offering—with this difference, that their ministrations and these commemorations do not send Christ our Lord to his life-giving passion.

26. They bring up the bread and place it on the holy altar to complete the representation of the passion. So from now on we should consider that Christ has already undergone the passion and is now placed on the altar as in a tomb. . . .

28. All this takes place amid general silence; for since the liturgy has not yet begun, it is appropriate that everyone should look on in fearful recollection and silent prayer while this great and august body is brought and laid out. . . .

PRAYER OVER THE OFFERINGS

30. Then comes the time for prayer aloud. The deacon announces it. He must be able to give the sign for the various ceremonies and explain their purpose. . . .

31. When he has performed his duty of arousing all the congregation and suggesting suitable prayers, everyone stands in silence while the bishop begins the Prayer Over the Offerings. We should address a prayer to God before any action that is connected with his service, especially this awesome liturgy which we can perform only with God's help.* In the course of the prayer he gives thanks to our Lord for the great favors he procured for the salvation and life of mankind, and for giving us knowledge of this wonderful sacrament which is the memorial of the sublime gift which he bestowed upon us through his passion—his promise that we should rise from the dead and ascend to heaven.

32. He gives thanks on his own behalf for the fact that Christ has made him a minister of so dread a sacrament. Then he makes this request, that God will grant him now the grace of the Holy Spirit by which he has been called to the priesthood, so that he may be worthy of his great ministry, and by the grace of God may be free from all evil intentions and fear of punishment, as he approaches these things that are infinitely beyond him.

33. When the bishop has concluded these prayers and others like them, all present reply: "Amen." This word is an exclamation of agreement with the bishop's prayer. St Paul mentions it: "How can any one in the position of an outsider say the 'Amen' to your thanksgiving when he does not know what you are saying . . ."

34. When the congregation has said "Amen," the bishop prays: "Peace be with you." It is a good practice to begin every ceremony in church with this phrase, especially the dread liturgy which is about to be celebrated. . . .

35. It has always been laid down that those who are privileged to perform the duties of a priest must begin every ceremony in church with this prayer, especially the celebration of the dread sacrament. The bishop's prayer that all may enjoy peace proclaims the wonderful blessings of which this liturgy of the memorial of our Lord's death is the sign and the means.* The congregation replies: "And with your spirit."

36. In return they make the same prayer for him, showing the bishop and all present that, while the others need the bishop's blessing and prayer, he in turn needs their prayer. For this reason it has always been the custom that the prayers of the Church should include the needs of bishops as well as those of the rest; for we are one body of Christ our Lord and all "members one of another." The bishop plays the part of a more important limb than the others. . . . * That is why at the word "peace" he blesses the congregation, and receives their blessing in turn when they say: "And with your spirit."

38. This is the reason for the ancient custom of the Church that the congregation should reply to the bishop: "And with thy spirit."

When all is well with the bishop, the whole body of the Church feels the benefit, but when he is ailing, the whole community suffers. So all pray that this "peace" will bring him the grace of the Holy Spirit to enable him to fulfil his duties and perform the liturgy worthily on behalf of the community. Conversely, the abundance of the grace of the Holy Spirit will give the bishop peace, making it easier for him to perform the prescribed ceremonies when in all his affairs and especially in the liturgy he shows that he has a clear conscience.

KISS OF PEACE

39.   When the bishop and the congregation have exchanged blessings, the bishop begins to give the Kiss of Peace, and the church herald, that is today, the deacon, in a loud voice orders all the people to exchange the Kiss of Peace, following the bishop's example. This kiss which all present exchange constitutes a kind of profession of the unity and charity that exists among them. Each of us gives the Kiss of Peace to the person next to him, and so in effect gives it to the whole assembly, because this act is an acknowledgment that we have all become the single body of Christ our Lord, and so must preserve with one another that harmony that exists among the limbs of a body, loving one another equally, supporting and helping one another regarding the individual's needs as concerns of the community, sympathizing with one another's sorrows and sharing in one another's joys.

40. The new birth that we underwent at baptism is unique for this reason, that it joins us into a natural unity; and so we all share the same food when we partake of the same body and the same blood, for we have been linked in the unity of baptism. St Paul says: "Because there is one loaf, we who are many are one body, for we all partake of the same loaf" (1 Cor 10.17). This is why before we approach the sacrament of the liturgy we are required to observe the custom of giving the Kiss of Peace, as a profession of unity and mutual charity. It would certainly not be right for those who form a single body, the body of the church, to entertain hatred toward a brother in the faith, who has shared the same birth so as to become a member of the same body, and whom we believe to be a member of Christ our Lord, just as we are, and to share the same food at the spiritual table. Our Lord said: "Every one who is angry with his brother without cause shall be liable to judgment" (Mt 5.22; alternative reading). This ceremony, then, is not only a profession of charity, but a reminder to us to lay aside all unholy enmity, if we feel that our cause of complaint against one of our brothers in the faith is not just. After our Lord had forbidden any unjust anger, he offered the following remedy to sinners of every kind: "If you are offering your gift at the altar, and there remember that your brother has something against you, leave your gift there before the altar and go; first be reconciled to your brother, and then come and offer your gift" (Mt 5.23–24). He tells the sinner to seek immediately every means of reconciliation with the man he has offended, and not to presume to make his offering until he has made amends to the one he has wronged and done all in his power to placate him; for we all make the offering by the agency of the bishop.

41. For although it is the bishop who stands up to make the offering, he is only acting as the tongue on behalf of the whole body. We all make the offering in common, and all derive from it a common benefit and to all is extended an equal share of what has been offered. When St Paul says of the high priest that "he is bound to offer sacrifice for his own sins as well as for those of the people" (Heb 5, 3), he implies that the high priest is appointed to make a common offering for himself and for everyone else.

If anyone has wronged another, then, he must do all he can to make amends to the one he has wronged and to effect a reconciliation with him. If the injured party is present, the reconciliation should be made on the spot; if not, the offender must resolve to seek a reconciliation by all the means in his power when occasion offers. Only then may he come forward to take part in the offering. The injured party, on the other hand, must accept the other's offer of redress as readily as the offender made it.* He must put out of his mind all memories of the wrongs done to him and recall our Lord's words: "If you do not forgive men their trespasses neither will your Father forgive your trespasses" (Mt 6.15). We must regard the Kiss of Peace as a profession and a reminder of all this. Like St Paul, we should give one another peace "with a holy kiss" (Rom 16.16); we must not be like Judas and kiss with the mouth only, while remaining set on showing hatred and malice to our brothers in the faith.

LAVABO

42. Next the bishop washes his hands, and after him all the priests present, however many there may be, do the same. They do not perform this ceremony to get their hands clean: decency requires that everyone should wash, priests on account of their ministry, others on account of the offering they are about to receive. But the priests are appointed to offer the sacrifice for the whole community, and so they perform this ceremony to remind us all that when the sacrifice is offered we must all offer ourselves with clean consciences. Accordingly immediately after the Kiss of Peace by which we profess that we have laid aside all hatred and bitterness against our brothers in the faith and washed away the memory of grudges, we need to cleanse ourselves from every stain.

COMMEMORATION OF THE LIVING AND THE DEAD

43. All stand at a sign from the deacon and fix their eyes on the actions that are performed. The names of the living and the dead who have died believing in Christ are read from the Church records. These short lists of names, of course, include implicitly all the living and the dead. We learn from this the effect of the incarnate life of Christ our Lord. For this liturgy, which is his memorial, benefits all, living and dead alike; the living contemplate their hopes for the future, while the dead are no longer dead but deep in sleep, waiting in the hope for which Christ our Lord accepted the death that we commemorate in this sacrament.

PREPARATION FOR THE EUCHARISTIC PRAYER

44. After the reading of these lists, the bishop comes forward to perform the liturgy, while the Church herald (i.e. the deacon who announces to the congregation how to follow the actions of the bishop) proclaims: "Turn you eyes to the offering."* For the ceremony which is about to take place is a community affair. The community sacrifice is immolated and the community offering is presented on behalf of all, for those absent as well as those present, in as much as they have shared the faith and been numbered as members of God's Church and lived out their lives in it. It is evident that "to present the offering' and 'to immolate the offering" are synonymous terms, for what is immolated and offered to God is, as it were, a dread victim. Thus, St Paul says, Christ "did this once for all when he offered up himself," "it is necessary for this priest also to have something to offer" (Heb 7.27; 8.23). So since our sacrifice is a representation of Christ's sacrifice, we call it the "offering" or the "presenting of the offering." This is why it is appropriate for the deacon to prepare the ceremony with the words: "Turn you eyes to the offering."

45. All have been warned to turn their eyes to the objects that have been placed in readiness. . . . Now the bishop begins the offering itself. How? You must be taught this too. But I have spoken for long enough: I shall keep this subject for another day, if God permits. And may God the Father, the Son and the Holy Spirit be praised for all things, now and for ever. Amen.

BAPTISMAL HOMILY—V

THE EUCHARISTIC PRAYER: INTRODUCTORY RESPONSES

2. As soon as the deacon says: "Turn your eyes to the offering," and all have obediently turned their eyes on the action taking place, *the bishop begins the Eucharistic Prayer. First he blesses the people with the words: "The grace of the Lord Jesus Christ and the love of God the Father and the fellowship of the Holy Spirit be with you all."* He knows that now, before the liturgy, more than at any other time, the people need to receive this apostolic blessing. It is so rich in meaning and so solemn in character that the bishop uses it as a beginning. . . . *The people reply: "And with your spirit."* As always when the bishop blesses the people, wishing them "grace" or "peace," custom requires all present to make the response that I have already explained.

3. After the blessing the bishop prepares the people for what is to come with the words: "Lift up your hearts". . .

4. The people reply: *"To you, O Lord,"* thus professing their willingness to comply. When the bishop has duly prepared the congregation's minds and hearts in this way, he says: *"Let us give thanks to the Lord"*. . . *the people reply: "It is right and fitting"*. . .

5. Then, when we are all standing in silence and profound awe, *the bishop proceeds to offer up the offering and immolate the sacrifice on behalf of the community.* He is filled with awe both for himself and for us because our Lord suffered death for us all, a death which will be commemorated in this sacrifice. At this moment the bishop is the tongue of all the Church. . . .

6. We were instructed and baptized in the name of the Father and of the Son and of the Holy Spirit, and to them we must turn for the fulfillment of what is performed in the liturgy. So now the bishop says: "The majesty of the Father," but adds the words: "And of the Son," because the Son stands to the Father as one who is truly a Son, is like the Father, has the same substance as he has, and is in no respect inferior to him.* The bishop must also add the name of the Holy Spirit, thus acknowledging that he too is the divine substance. All creation the bishop says, and especially the invisible powers, ever praise and glorify this divine, eternally existing nature. He makes special mention of the Seraphim who raise this hymn of praise to God. . . . *"Holy, holy, holy is the Lord of hosts. His praise fill all heaven and earth."*

7. . . . because scripture describes them singing the hymn of praise that all of us recite in a loud voice, paying our worship to God, in company with the invisible powers.*. . .

9. As for us . . . we stand *with eyes cast down* in such great reverence that we cannot even look upon the majesty of this liturgy. We make the words of the invisible powers our own to express the greatness of the mercy which has been unexpectedly lavished upon us. The feeling of awe does not leave us; throughout the liturgy, both before and after the exclamation "Holy," we keep our eyes on the ground.

10. When all present have exclaimed: *"Holy, holy, holy" and fallen silent again,* the bishop continues the liturgy. First he says: "Holy is the Father, holy is the Son, holy is the Holy Spirit." These words are a profession of faith in this holy and eternal nature and a proof that he has interpreted the hymn of the Seraphim accurately. Then he proclaims the transcendent mercy that God bestowed on us when he revealed his plan for us in Christ. For Christ, "though he was in the form of God," determined to "take the form of a servant" (Phil 2.6–7); he assumed a perfect and complete man for the salvation of the human race, thus canceling the ancient and cruel burdens of the law and death's long-established hold over us, and conferring upon us favors beyond our description or comprehension. For Christ our Lord accepted the passion in order to exterminate death utterly by his resurrection; and he has promised that we too can share with him in the enjoyment of this future.

So it was necessary for Christ to give us this mystery with its power to lead on to our future. Through it we are born again in the sign of baptism, commemorate our Lord's death by this dread liturgy, and receive his body and blood as our immortal and spiritual food. When he was about to go to meet his passion, he bequeathed this food to his disciples, so that we might receive his body and blood by means of this bread and wine—we who all believe in Christ and continue to commemorate his death. . . .

EPICLESIS OVER THE OFFERING

11. . . . *But by virtue of the sacramental actions, this is the moment appointed for "Christ our Lord to rise from the dead and pour out his grace upon us all."* This can take place only by the coming of the Holy Spirit, by which the Holy Spirit once raised Christ from the dead.

12. Accordingly, the bishop is obliged by the liturgical rules to entreat God that the Holy Spirit may come and that grace may descend from on high to the bread and wine that have been offered, so showing us that the memorial of immortality is truly the body and blood of our Lord. For our Lord's body is of the same nature as ours: it was originally by nature mortal but by means of the resurrection passed to an immortal and unchanging nature. . . . Just as our Lord's body was clearly revealed as

immortal when it had received the Spirit and his anointing, so too in the liturgy the bread and wine that have been offered receive at the coming of the Holy Spirit a kind of anointing by grace that comes upon them. From this moment we believe that they are the body and blood of Christ, free from death, corruption, suffering and change, like our Lord's body after the resurrection.

EPICLESIS OVER THE PEOPLE

13. *The bishop also prays that the grace of the Holy Spirit may come upon all the assembly.* The new birth has made them grow into a single body; now they are to be firmly established in the one body by sharing the body of our Lord, and form a single unity in harmony, peace and good works. Thus we shall look upon God with a pure heart; we shall not incur punishment by communicating in the Holy Spirit when we are divided in our views, inclined to arguments, quarrels, envy and jealousy, and contemptuous of virtue. By our harmony, peace and good works, and by the purity of heart with which our soul looks upon God, we shall show that we are waiting to receive the Holy Spirit. In this way, by communion in the blessed mysteries, we shall be united among ourselves and joined to Christ our Lord, whose body we believe ourselves to be, and through whom we "become partakers of the divine nature" (2 Pet 1.4).

COMMEMORATION OF THE LIVING AND THE DEAD

14. The bishop performs the divine liturgy in this way, and *offers a prayer for all whom it is always customary to name in church; and then passes on to the commemoration of the dead.* For this sacrifice obtains protection for us in this world, and on those who have died in the faith it confers after death fulfilment of that transcendent hope which is the desire of the goal of all the children of Christ's mystery.

15. *After these prayers the bishop pauses, then takes the sacred bread in his hands and looks up to heaven,* directing his gaze upward as an expression of thanks for such marvelous gifts. Then *he breaks the bread,* at the same time *praying for the people that the grace of Jesus*

Christ may come upon them . . . The people reply in the usual way expressing agreement. *He traces the sign of the cross over the blood with the bread and over the bread with the blood.* He brings them together as a sign that, though they are two distinct things, they are one in power and are the memorial of the passion and death that affected our Lord's body when he shed his blood on the cross for us all. . . .

16. When our Lord gave his body and blood, he said: "This is my body which is broken for you for the forgiveness of sins," and "This is my blood which is shed for you for the remission of sins." The first saying referred to his passion, the second to the cruelty and length of it, which caused so much blood to be shed. So it is appropriate that we too should follow this tradition and set both bread and wine on the altar as a sign of what took place and as a reminder that the two are one in power, because both belong to the one who underwent the passion—i.e., both the body of our Lord and the blood that was shed from it. . . .

17. *For this reason it is laid down that he should drop the life-giving bread piece by piece into the chalice.* This action shows that the two elements are inseparable, that they are one in power and that they confer one and the same grace on the receiver.

18. This is why the bishop, now that he has duly completed the liturgy, follows our Lord's example—for this is the memorial of his death and resurrection—and breaks the bread just as our Lord shared himself out in his appearances, appearing to different people at different times, and finally to a great gathering. In this way everyone was able to come to him. So too now people have a high regard for the gift that has been revealed to them; they adore our Lord and acknowledge the great reward that came to him; and they receive him in their hearts by eating the consecrated bread so that they too may enjoy sublime communion with him. With great delight and joy and in strong hopes we are led this way to the greatness which through the resurrection we hope to experience with him in the world to come.

19. Eventually, then, all the bread is broken, so that all of us who are present can receive a share. When we receive one little mouth-

ful, we believe that in this mouthful we each receive Christ whole. For it would be scandalous if the woman with the flow of blood received a divine favor simply by touching the fringe of his garment (Lk 8.43ff), not even part of his body, while we believed that we did not receive him whole in a fragment of his body. Again, when we kiss, we ordinarily do so with the mouth; it is a small part of the body, but by means of it we intend to embrace the whole body. We often walk in pairs hand in hand, taking this part of the body as a sign of our fellowship.

20. With a view to what is to happen afterward, the bishop who offers this sacred, sublime sacrifice must begin by performing the same action; when he has concluded the liturgy of consecration, he begins to break the bread. This is an appropriate action; from this point we must picture Christ our Lord in our minds by means of this bread, for in each one of the fragments he comes to the receiver. He greets us and reveals his resurrection and gives us a guarantee of the promised blessings. . . .

21. When all this has been done, the church herald speaks out again and reminds us briefly of those for whom we should all pray. First he announces: *"We must pray for the one who has brought this holy offering."* That is to say, we have been granted the privilege of making this offering; let us continue to pray that we may become worthy of looking at it and staying close to it and sharing in it. The bishop concludes the prayer by asking that God may approve of the sacrifice and that the grace of the Holy Spirit may come upon the world, so that we may not be punished for sharing in the sacrament, although it is infinitely above us.*

22. When the bishop has concluded the Eucharistic Prayer in this way, *he blesses the people and wishes them peace; all present make the usual response with heads bowed in due reverence.* When the prayer is completed and all are intent on receiving Holy Communion, *the church herald proclaims: "Let us attend"* . . . *The bishop announces: "What is holy for the holy."* "For our Lord's body and blood, which are our food, are indeed holy and immortal and full of holiness, since the Holy Spirit has come down upon them." Not everyone may receive this food, but only those who have been sanctified, and therefore only the baptized who have undergone a new birth,

and "have the first fruits of the Holy Spirit" (Rom 8.23), which enables them to receive the favor of sanctification. This is why the bishop says: "What is holy to the holy," and urges everyone to recall the dignity of what is laid on the altar. . . .

23. . . . You must lead good lives so as to strengthen in your own persons the gift which has been given you and to be worthy of the food you require.*. . . You too have been born in baptism by the grace of the Holy Spirit and his coming and received this sanctification; accordingly you need to receive food of the same kind by the grace and the coming of the Holy Spirit, so that this sanctification you have been given may be strengthened and grow, and the promised blessing may be fulfilled in the world to come where we shall all enjoy complete holiness. This is the meaning of "What is holy for the holy." With these dispositions, with this profession of faith, with this eagerness, we approach this sublime communion; we must receive this holy, immortal food in fear combined with love.

This is what the bishop's words mean. *All reply: "One holy Father, one holy Son, one Holy Spirit,"* acknowledging that there is only one holy nature, the nature of the Father, the Son and the Holy Spirit; alone it exists from all eternity, alone it is unchanging, alone it can confer sanctification on whoever it wills. *They add: "Glory be to the Father and to the Son and to the Holy Spirit for ever and ever. Amen."* For all who acknowledge the holy nature owe it a debt of praise.

COMMUNION

24. Once the liturgy has been concluded in this way, *then we all eagerly receive the offering.* We receive from the dread ineffable altar an immortal and holy food. Those who have charge of the divine liturgy and stand near the altar approach it to receive the divine food; the others receive away from the altar. But this makes no difference to the food itself; for there is only one bread, and only one body of Christ our Lord into which the bread that has been offered is transformed by the one coming of the Holy Spirit, and we all receive it equally because we are the one body of Christ our Lord and are all nourished with the same body and blood. . . . St

Paul teaches us that when we receive them, we are united with our Lord's body and blood, and so remain in communion with him and are ourselves Christ's body, while this communion strengthens the communion we received by the new birth of baptism. We have become his body. St Paul said "*You* are the body of Christ," and again: Christ is "the Head, from whom the whole body, nourished and knit together, grows with a growth that is from God" (1 Cor 12.27; Col 2.19). . . .

26. Now by means of these commemorations and signs that have been performed, we all approach the risen Christ with great delight. We embrace him as joyfully as we can, for we see him risen from the dead and hope ourselves to attain to a share in the resurrection. In the symbols that have been enacted, he rose out of the dead from the altar, as if from a tomb; he appears and comes close to us; and when we receive him in communion, he announces to us his resurrection. Although he shares himself when he comes to us, he is entire in each part and close to each of us, giving himself to each of us for us to seize and embrace him with all our might and show him whatever love we choose to give. . . .

27. *Then we each come forward, with eyes cast down and hands extended.* By our lowered eyes we pay the debt of fitting adoration, making a public act of faith that we are receiving the body of the King who became Lord of all by union with the divine nature and is worshiped as Lord by all creatures alike. Our two hands stretched out together acknowledge the value of the gift we are about to receive. *The right hand is stretched out to receive the offering, and the left hand underneath.* This is a sign of great reverence: the right hand is stretched out uppermost because it is to receive the royal body; the other hand supports and guides its sister and partner, for it is not ashamed to play the part of a servant to its equal in deference to the royal body that the right hand is carrying.

28. *As he gives communion, the bishop says: "The body of Christ."* These words teach you not to pay attention to the appearance, but to put yourself in mind of what has happened to the offering, which by the coming of the Holy Spirit has become the body of Christ. You should come up in great fear and with much love because of the greatness of the gift—fear because of its great dignity, love because of its grace. *So you say "Amen" to his words,* confirming and subscribing to the bishop's declaration. *You receive the chalice in the same way.*

When you have received the body in your hands, you adore it, acknowledging the authority of him who is placed in your hands and recalling our Lord's words to his disciples after his resurrection: "Authority in heaven and on earth has been given to me" (Mt 28.18). With a great and sincere love you place it on your eyes, kiss it and address to it your prayers as to Christ our Lord who is now with you, for you possess the great source of confidence you hoped for, now that you have come to him and taken hold of him. As you pray you confess your weakness and your many sins, and acknowledge that you are utterly undeserving of such a gift; you pay him the glory that is his due for giving you these gifts and for favoring you with such help that, by becoming free from all evil and always performing his will, you have become worthy of receiving the offering.

29. In such dispositions as these you receive and swallow your share in the sacrament. The grace of the Holy Spirit does not only feed the body; by this dread communion it also feeds the soul as well as the body, and even more than the body; when it makes the body immortal in the world to come, it also makes the soul immune to change and to all sin. *After you have received, you offer up on your own account the thanksgiving and blessing that are due to God,* so as not to be ungrateful for this divine gift, *remaining with all the congregation to pay this debt of thanksgiving and blessing in accordance with the Church's custom.* For it is only right that all who have received this spiritual food should give thanks to God in common for this great gift. . . .

44. . . . With this end in view we have obtained by God's grace the favor of celebrating this mystery now, and of enjoying the kingdom of heaven and all the indescribable blessings which will last for ever and which we shall all receive by the grace of our Lord Jesus Christ. To him with the Father and the Holy Spirit be glory now and for ever. Amen.

CHAPTER FIFTEEN

EGERIA'S *DIARY OF A PILGRIMAGE*

The following selection differs from any preceding it because it is neither a liturgical text nor a homiletic exposition of the meaning of the rites of initiation. It is an **Itinerarium,** *a travel diary, which in recent years has attracted a great deal of attention, particularly of historians of liturgy, because of its description of the liturgy of the church in Jerusalem at the end of the fourth and the beginning of the fifth centuries. The Latin manuscript, substantial but incomplete, was discovered in 1884 in Arezzo, Italy, and its origin traced to the Benedictine monastery of Monte Cassino. The consensus among contemporary scholars attributes the* **Diary** *to a devout woman, probably a nun, who was writing to a group of fellow religious in her homeland, Galicia in northwestern Spain, in the early years of the fifth century. The text has two major sections. Chapters 1–23 describe several pilgrimages to places in Egypt, Palestine and Syria that were of biblical or traditional importance. The remaining 26 chapters describe the religious and liturgical life of Jerusalem. Obviously a curious, devout woman of considerable resources, her* **Diary** *is uniquely descriptive. The sections which appear here describe the procedures during Lent as the "elect" prepared for baptism and, more briefly, the postbaptismal period of instruction. In these sections Egeria mentions two of the six churches of Jerusalem, the Martyrium and the Anastasis. The former was the major church of Jerusalem, "because" as she explains, "it is on Golgotha, behind the cross, where the Lord suffered His Passion, and is therefore a shrine of martyrdom" (30). The latter was the sanctuary of the Resurrection, a church constructed in the round, in the center of which was the grotto of the Holy Sepulchre or tomb of the Lord. As described here, Jerusalem's eight-week Lenten preparation for baptism was carried out with great care under the supervision of the bishop. Egeria points out to her sisters that the Easter vigil was observed in Jerusalem "exactly as we observe it at home" (38). The following points in Egeria's account*

may be noted. The "elect" or "competentes" are enrolled on the day before Lent begins. The bishop assumes a central role in the process. He inquires of the community about the character of each candidate as Lent begins and he himself inscribes their names in the register. He provides the catechetical instruction in "the law" explaining both the "literal" and "spiritual" sense of scripture to the candidates and any of the faithful, in addition to the sponsors, who wanted to attend. Catechumens, whose initiation was deferred, were excluded. As Egeria notes, the daily three-hour instruction permitted all of the faithful to understand the scriptures when they were read in the Liturgy. An explanation of the articles of the Creed (traditio symboli) followed the instruction in scriptures. In Holy Week the candidates were expected to recite the Creed in the bishop's presence (reditio symboli). In Jerusalem, as the Egeria explains and the catechectical homilies of Cyril confirm, the multilingual instruction prior to baptism did not include Baptism or the Eucharist, which were explained only during Easter week after the sacraments had been received.
[Translation: ACW, 38, pp. 113–114, 122–126]

DIARY OF A PILGRIMAGE

CHAPTER 38

. . . The Easter vigil is observed here exactly as we observe it at home. Only one thing is done more elaborately here. After the neophytes have been baptized and dressed as soon as they come forth from the baptismal font, they are led first of all to the Anastasis with the bishop. The bishop goes within the railings of the Anastasis, a hymn is sung, and he prays for them. Then he returns with them to the major church, where all the people are holding the vigil as is customary.

Everything is done which is customarily done at home with us, and after the sacrifice has been offered, the dismissal is given. After the vigil service has been celebrated in the major church, everyone comes to the Anastasis singing hymns. There, once again, the text of the Gospel of the Resurrection is read, a prayer is said, and once again the bishop offers the sacrifice. However, for the sake of the people, everything is done rapidly, lest they be delayed too long. And so the people are dismissed. On this day the dismissal from the vigil takes place at the same hour as at home with us.

CHAPTER 45

I must also describe how those who are baptized at Easter are instructed. Whoever gives his name does so the day before Lent, and the priest notes down all their names; and this is before those eight weeks during which, as I have said, Lent is observed here. When the priest has noted down everyone's name, then, on the following day, the first day of Lent, on which the eight weeks begin, a throne is set up for the bishop in the center of the major church, the Martyrium. The priests sit on stools on both sides, and all the clergy stand around. One by one the candidates are led forward, in such a way that the men come with their godfathers and the women with their godmothers.

Then the bishop questions individually the neighbors of the one who has come up, inquiring: "Does he lead a good life? Does he obey his parents? Is he a drunkard or liar?" And he seeks out in the man other vices which are more serious. If the person proves to be guiltless in all these matters concerning which the bishop has questioned the witnesses who are present, he notes down the man's name with his own hand. If, however, he is accused of anything, the bishop orders him to go out and says: "Let him amend his life, and when he has done so, let him then approach the baptismal font." He makes the same inquiry of both men and women. If, however, someone is a stranger, he cannot easily receive baptism, unless he has witnesses who know him.

CHAPTER 46

Ladies, my sisters, I must describe this, lest you think that it is done without explanation. It is the custom here, throughout the forty days on which there is fasting, for those who are preparing for baptism to be exorcized by the clergy early in the morning, as soon as the dismissal from the morning service has been given at the Anastasis. Immediately a throne is placed for the bishop in the major church, the Martyrium. All those who are to be baptized, both men and women, sit closely around the bishop, while the godmothers and godfathers stand there; and indeed all of the people who wish to listen may enter and sit down, provided they are of the faithful. A catechumen, however, may not enter at the time when the bishop is teaching them the law. He does so in this way: beginning with Genesis he goes through the whole of Scripture during these forty days, expounding first its literal meaning and then explaining the spiritual meaning. In the course of these days everything is taught not only about the Resurrection but concerning the body of faith. This is called catechetics.

When five weeks of instruction have been completed, they then receive the Creed. He explains the meaning of each of the phrases of the Creed in the same way he explained Holy Scripture, expounding first the literal and then the spiritual sense. In this fashion the Creed is taught.

And thus it is that in these places all the faithful are able to follow the Scriptures when they are read in the churches, because all are taught through those forty days, that is, from the first to the third hours, for during the three hours instruction is given. God knows, ladies, my sisters, that the voices of the faithful who have come to catechetics to hear instruction on those things being said or explained by the bishop are louder than when the bishop sits down in church to preach about each of those matters which are explained in this fashion. The dismissal from catechetics is given at the third hour, and immediately, singing hymns, they lead the bishop to the Anastasis, and the office of the third hour takes place. And thus they are taught for three hours a day for seven weeks. During the eighth week, the one which is called the Great Week, there remains no more time for them to be taught, because what has been mentioned above must be carried out.

Now when seven weeks have gone by and there remains only Holy Week, which is here called the Great Week, then the bishop comes in the morning to the major church, the Martyrium. To the rear, at the apse behind the altar, a throne is placed for the bishop, and one by one they come forth, the men with their godfathers, the women with their godmothers. And each one recites the Creed back to the bishop. After the Creed has been recited back to the bishop, he delivers a homily to them all, and says: "During these seven weeks you have heard about the faith. You have also heard of the resurrection of the flesh. But as for the whole explanation of the Creed, you have heard only that which you are able to know while you are still catechumens. Because you are still catechumens, you are not able to know those things which belong to a still higher mystery, that of baptism. But that you may not think that anything would be done without explanation, once you have been baptized in the name of God, you will hear them during the eight days of Easter in the Anastasis following the dismissal from church. Because you are still catechumens, the most secret of the divine mysteries cannot be told to you."

CHAPTER 47

When it is Easter week, during the eight days from Easter Sunday to its octave, as soon as the dismissal has been given from the church, everyone, singing hymns, goes to the Anastasis. Soon a prayer is said, the faithful are blessed, and the bishop stands up. Leaning on the inner railing, which is in the grotto of the Anastasis, he explains everything which is accomplished in baptism. At this hour no catechumen goes into the Anastasis; only the neophytes and the faithful who wish to hear the mysteries enter the Anastasis. Indeed, the doors are closed, lest any catechumen come that way. While the bishop is discussing and explaining each point, so loud are the voices of praise that they can be heard outside the church. And he explains all these mysteries in such a manner that there is no one who would not be drawn to them, when he heard them thus explained.

A portion of the population in this province knows both Greek and Syriac, another segment knows only Greek; and still another, only Syriac. Even though the bishop may know Syriac, he always speaks Greek and never Syriac; and, therefore, there is always present a priest who, while the bishop speaks in Greek, translates into Syriac, so that all may understand what is being explained. Since whatever scriptural texts are read must be read in Greek, there is always someone present who can translate the readings into Syriac for the people. So that those here who are Latins, those consequently knowing neither Greek nor Syriac, will not be bored, everything is explained to them, for there are other brothers and sisters who are bilingual in Greek and Latin and who explain everything to them in Latin. But this above all is very pleasing and admirable here, that whatever hymns and antiphons are sung, whatever readings and prayers are recited by the bishop, they are said in such a manner as to be proper and fitting to the feast which is being observed and to the place where the service is being held.

CHAPTER SIXTEEN

THE LETTER OF JOHN THE DEACON

John the Deacon, possibly the later Pope John I, in his letter to Senarius, a Roman nobleman and probably a member of the court of Theodoric, provides an explanation rather than a description of the rites of initiation as observed at the beginning of the sixth century in Rome. John's explanation bears comparison with the rites as contained in **The Apostolic Tradition** *of Hippolytus and as explained by Ambrose of Milan, who insisted that in all things he desired "to follow the Church in Rome"* **(De Sac.** *III, 5). Attention in the excerpts focuses primarily upon the explanation of the rites accompanying the formation of candidates in the "classroom of the catechumens." John describes the repeated laying on of hands, exorcisms, and exsufflation (the minister breathes upon the catechumen as though to blow the devil away), the giving of the salt as a preservative from evil influences, and the giving of the Creed to the catechumens. With the reception of the Creed, the catechumens enter into the ranks of the elect and, as John points out, begin to live within the womb of Mother Church, whence they shall be reborn in the waters of baptism. The "scrutinies," which take place in the final weeks of preparation, have as their purpose to ascertain the faith development of those preparing for baptism. John also describes the rite of anointing the ears and nostrils of the catechumens, a rite which is found only in Rome and Milan. In Rome at the time of Hippolytus, the rite appears to have taken place immediately prior to baptism and to have been fused with a prebaptismal anointing, while at Milan "the opening," which also took place on Holy Saturday, was not accompanied by an anointing with oil. It is interesting to note that by the beginning of the sixth century the rite of baptismal anointing, which as Hippolytus described it earlier involved the bishop liberally anointing the body of the catechumen from his cupped hand, has diminished to a simple sign of the cross on the breast. As in the rites of initiation familiar to Tertullian in Africa as well as to Hippolytus in Rome, the neophytes drank from a chalice of milk and honey,*

signifying their entrance into the promised land, at their first Eucharist.
Finally, it may be pointed out that despite the similarities in the rites of
the third and sixth centuries, John thinks it necessary to say that
although the old books may show no traces of some of the rites, the
Church has prescribed them with watchful care over many years.
Tradition provides the necessary continuity.
[Translation, Whitaker, pp. 144–148]

LETTER TO SENARIUS

2. You ask me to tell you why before a man is baptized he must
first become a catechumen; or what the meaning of the word is or
of the word "catechizing"; in what rule of the Old Testament it is
set out; or whether indeed the rule is a new one, deriving rather
from the New Testament. Also you ask what a scrutiny is, and
why infants are scrutinized three times before the Pascha: and what
purpose is served by this care and preoccupation with these
examinations.

3. Here is my reply. I am confident that you are sufficiently versed
in such matters to know that the whole human race, while still so
to speak in its cradle, should properly have fallen in death through
the waywardness of the first man, and no rescue was possible
except by the grace of the Saviour, who although he had been
begotten of the Father before the worlds yet for our salvation did
not disdain to be born in time, man of a virgin mother alone.
There cannot therefore be any doubt that before a man is reborn
in Christ he is held close in the power of the devil, and unless he
is extricated from the devil's toils, renouncing him among the first
beginnings of faith with a true confession, he cannot approach the
grace of the saving laver. And therefore he must first enter the
classroom of the catechumens. *Catechesis* is the Greek word for
instruction. He is instructed through the Church's ministry, by the
blessing of one laying his hand [upon his head] that he may know
who he is and who he shall be: in other words, that from being one
of the damned he becomes holy, from unrighteousness he appears
as righteous, and finally, from being a servant he becomes a son, so
that a man whose first parentage brought him perdition is restored
by the gift of a second parentage, and becomes the possessor of a
father's inheritance. He receives therefore exsufflation and exor-

cism, in order that the devil may be put to flight and an entrance prepared for Christ our God: so that being delivered from the power of darkness, he may be *translated to the kingdom* (Col 1.13) of the glory of the love of God: so that a man who till recently had been a vessel of Satan becomes now a dwelling of the Savior. And so he receives exsufflation, because the old deceiver merits such ignominy. He is exorcized, however, that is to say he is adjured to go out and depart and acknowledge the approach of him whose upright image he had cast down in the bliss of Paradise by his wicked counsel. The catechumen receives blessed salt also, to signify that just as all flesh is kept healthy by salt, so the mind which is drenched and weakened by the waves of this world is held steady by the salt of wisdom and of the preaching of the word of God: so that it may come to stability and permanence, after the distemper of corruption is thoroughly settled by the gentle action of the divine salt. This then is achieved by frequent laying on of the hand, and by the blessing of his Creator called over his head three times in honor of the Trinity.

4. And so by efforts of himself and others the man who had recently received exsufflation and had renounced the toils and pomps of the devil is next permitted to receive the words of the Creed [symbolum] which was handed down by the Apostles: so that he who a short time before was called simply a cathechumen may now be called a competent, or elect. For he was conceived in the womb of Mother Church and now he begins to live, even though the time of the sacred birth is not yet fulfilled. Then follow those occasions which according to the Church's custom are commonly called scrutinies. For we scrutinize their hearts through faith, to ascertain whether since the renunciation of the devil the sacred words have fastened themselves on his mind: whether they acknowledge the future grace of the Redeemer: whether they confess that they believe in God the Father Almighty. And when by their replies it becomes clear that it is so, according as it is written: "With the heart man believes unto righteousness, but with the mouth confession is made unto salvation" (Rom 10.10). Their ears are touched with the oil of sanctification, and their nostrils are also touched: the ears because through them faith enters the mind, according as the apostle says: "Faith comes by hearing, and hearing

by the word of God" (Rom 10.17): so that, the ears being as it were fortified by a kind of wall of sanctification, may permit entrance to nothing harmful, nothing which might entice them back.

5. When their nostrils are touched, they are thus without doubt admonished that for as long as they draw the breath of life through their nostrils they must abide in the service and the commandments of God. Whence that holy man says: "As God lives, who has taken away my judgment: and the Almighty who has vexed my soul; all the while my breath is in me, and the Spirit of God is in my nostrils; my lips should not speak wickedness nor my tongue utter deceit" (Job 27.2–4). The unction of the nostrils signifies this also, that since the oil is blessed in the Name of the Savior, they may be led unto his spiritual odor by the inner perception of a certain ineffable sweetness, so that in delight they may sing: "Thy name is as ointment poured forth: we shall run after the savior of thine ointments" (Song 1.3). And so the nostrils, being fortified by this mystery, can give no admittance to the pleasures of this world, nor anything which might weaken their minds.

6. Next the oil of consecration is used to anoint their breast, in which is the seat and dwelling place of the heart; so that they may understand that they promise with a firm mind and a pure heart eagerly to follow after the commandments of Christ, now that the devil has been driven out. They are bidden to go in naked even down to their feet, so that having put aside the carnal garments of mortality they may acknowledge that they make their journey upon a road upon which nothing harsh and nothing harmful can be found. The Church has ordained these things with watchful care over many years, although the old books may not show traces of them. And then when the elect or catechumen has advanced in faith by these spiritual conveyances, so to speak, it is necessary to be consecrated in the baptism of the one laver, in which sacrament his baptism is effected by a threefold immersion. And rightly so: for whoever comes to be baptized in the Name of the Trinity must signify that Trinity in a threefold immersion, and must acknowledge his debt to the bounty of him who upon the third day rose from the dead. He is next arrayed in white vesture, and his head

anointed with the unction of the sacred chrism: that the baptized person may understand that in his person kingdom and priestly mystery have met. For priests and princes used to be anointed with the oil of chrism, priests that they might offer sacrifices to God, princes that they might rule their people. For a fuller expression of the idea of priesthood, the head of the neophyte is dressed in a linen array: for priests of that time used always to deck the head with a certain mystic covering. All the neophytes are arrayed in white vesture to symbolize the resurgent Church, just as our Lord and Savior himself in the sight of certain disciples and prophets was thus transfigured on the mount, so that it was said: "His face did shine as the sun: his raiment was made white as snow" (Mt 127.2). This prefigured for the future the splendor of the resurgent Church, of which it is written: "Who is this that rises up" (Song 3.6) all in white? And so they wear white raiment so that though the ragged dress of ancient error has darkened the infancy of their first birth, the costume of their second birth should display the raiment of glory, so that clad in a wedding garment he may approach the table of the heavenly bridegroom as a new man.

7. I must say plainly and at once, in case I seem to have overlooked the point, that all these things are done even to infants, who by reason of their youth understand nothing. And by this you may know that when they are presented by their parents or others, it is necessary that their salvation should come through other people's profession, since their damnation came by another's fault.
. . .

12. You ask why milk and honey are placed in a most sacred cup and offered with the sacrifice at the Paschal Sabbath. The reason is that it is written in the Old Testament and in a figure promised to the New People: "I shall lead you into a land of promise, a land flowing with milk and honey" (Lev 20.24). The land of promise, then, is the land of resurrection to everlasting bliss, it is nothing else than the land of our body, which in the resurrection of the dead shall attain to the glory of incorruption and peace. This kind of sacrament, then, is offered to the newly baptized so that they may realize that no others but they, who partake of the Body and Blood of the Lord, shall receive the land of promise, and as they

start upon the journey thither, they are nourished like little children with milk and honey, so that they may sing: "How sweet are thy words unto my mouth, O Lord, sweeter than honey and the honeycomb" (Pss 119.103; 19.11). As new men therefore, abandoning the bitterness of sin, they drink milk and honey, so that they who in their first birth were nourished with the milk of corruption and first shed tears of bitterness, in their second birth may taste the sweetness of milk and honey in the bowels of the Church, so that being nourished upon such sacraments they may be dedicated to the mysteries of perpetual incorruption.

INDEX AND SURVEY OF
THE RITES OF INITIATION

Both because of its length and ready availability, the only part of the contemporary *RCIA* included in this collection is the "Third Stage: Celebration of the Sacraments of Initiation." With the exception of the "Ephphetha," which Ambrose describes as a preliminary rite to the celebration of the sacraments and which the contemporary RCIA (see n. 202) places within the Period of Purification and Enlightenment (ordinarily, the season of Lent), and "The Washing of Feet," which is peculiar to Ambrose, the index follows the order of rites of the *RCIA*. In this way the sources of the contemporary rite and the meaning of its various ritual acts as described by Cyril, Chrysostom and Ambrose, and Theodore will be more apparent than in an alphabetical index. The rites of initiation in antiquity varied from place to place and from time to time. Nevertheless, it is clear that the similarity among the various rites is greater than the differences. One source of possible confusion may be noted at this point. The early church made more extensive use of anointings than the contemporary church and it is difficult at times to distinguish the precise meaning of any one particular anointing. The distinction of one anointing from another, as is attempted below, is quite tentative.

[Abbreviations: *D*, Didache; *A*, First Apology of Justin; *AT*, The Apostolic Tradition of Hippolytus; *E*, Euchologion of Serapion; *AC*, Apostolic Constitutions; *A1*, Anaphora of Basil, *A2*, Anaphora of John Chrysostum; *RC*, Roman Canon; *RCIA*, Rite of Christian Initiation of Adults; *M* (1–5), Mystagogical Lectures of Cyril of Jerusalem; *BI2*, Second Baptismal Instruction of John Chrysostom; *S* (1–4), the De Sacramentis of Ambrose of Milan; *T* (1–5), Baptismal Homilies of Theodore of Mopsuestia; *AM*, Anaphora of Addai and Mari; L, Letter of the Deacon John.]

BAPTISM

1. The Opening (Ephphetha)
   St. Ambrose, *S1*, 2; pp. 132–133.

2. Renunciation
   Hippolytus, *AT*, p. 17.
   AC, pp. 53–54.
   Cyril, *M1*, 2–10; pp. 101–104.
   Chrysostom, *BI2*, 18–21; pp. 126–127.
   Ambrose, *S1*, 5–8; pp. 133–134.
   Theodore, *T2*, 5–12; pp. 153–154
   RCIA, 223–226; pp. 139–142.

3. Contract with Christ
   AC, p. 54.
   Cyril, *M1*, 9; p. 104.
   Chrysostom, *BI2*, 17, 21; pp. 126–127.
   Theodore, *T2*, 13–16; pp. 154–155.

4. First Anointing
   Hippolytus, *AT*, p. 26.
   Serapion, *E*, p. 47.
   Chrysostom, *BI2*, 22–24; pp. 127–128.
   Cyril, *M2*, 3; p. 105.
   Ambrose, *S1*, 4; p. 133.
   Theodore, *T2*, 17–19; p. 156.
   John, *L*, 6; 188.

5. Stripping
   Hippolytus, *AT*, p. 25.
   Cyril, *M2*, 2; p. 105.
   Chrysostom, *BI2*, 24; p. 128.
   Theodore, *T2*, 19; p. 156.
   John, *L*, 6; p. 190.

6. Second Anointing
   Hippolytus, *AT*, p. 27.
   Serapion, *E*, pp. 49–50.
   Theodore, *T3*, 8; p. 159.

7. Blessing of the Font
   Serapion, *E*, pp. 45–46.
   AC, p. 55.
   Ambrose, *S1*, 15–19; pp. 136–137.
   Theodore, *T3*, 9–10; pp. 159–160.
   RCIA, pp. 89–91.

8. Baptism (Profession of Faith, Immersion, Trinitarian Formula)
   Didache, p. 12.
   Justin, *A*, 61; pp. 16–17.
   Hippolytus, *AT*, pp. 26–27.
   Cyril, *M2*, 4–7; pp. 105–107.
   Chrysostom, *BI2*, 25–26; pp. 128.
   Ambrose, *S2*, 20–24; pp. 139–141.
   Theodore, *T3*, 11–22; pp. 160–163.
   John, *L*, 6; pp. 190–191.
   RCIA, pp. 92–93.

9. The Washing of the Feet
   Ambrose, *S3*, 4–7; pp. 142–143.

10. The White Garment
    Cyril, *M4*, 8; p. 112.
    Theodore, *T3*, 26; p. 164.
    John, *L*, 6; p. 191.
    RCIA, p. 94.

11. Anointing/Confirmation
    Hippolytus, *AT*, p. 28.
    Serapion, *E*, pp. 49–50.
    AC, p. 55.
    Cyril, *M3*, 1–7; pp. 107–110.

THE EUCHARIST

2. Narration of God's great deeds
    Addai and Mari, *AM*, p. 36.
    Basil, *A1*, p. 56–57.

3. Institution Narrative
    Hippolytus, *AT*, p. 31.
    Serapion, *E*, p. 41–42.
    AC, p. 60–62.
    Basil, *A1*, p. 57.
    Chrysostum, *A2*, pp. 59–60.
    Ambrose, *S4*, 21–23; p. 148.

4. Epiclesis
    Addai and Mari, *AM*, p. 37.
    Hippolytus, *AT*, p. 32.
    Serapion, *E*, pp. 42–43.
    Basil, *A1*, p. 58.
    Cyril, *M5*, 7; p. 115.
    Theodore, *T5*, 11–12; p. 174.

5. Anamnesis
    Hippolytus, *AT*, p. 31.
    Addai and Mari, *AM*, pp. 36.
    AC, p. 62.
    Basil, *A1*, p. 57.
    Chrysostum, *A2*, p. 60.
    Ambrose, *S*, 27; p. 149.

6. Prayer of offering
    Ambrose, *S4*, 27; p. 149.

7. Epiclesis over the people
    Hippolytus, *AT*, 32.
    AC, pp. 62–63.
    Theodore, *T5*, 13; p. 174.

8. Mementos of the living and dead
    Serapion, *E*, 43.
    Chrysostum, *A*, 61.

Cyril, *M*, 8–10; pp. 115–116.
Theodore, *T4*, 43; pp. 170–171; *T5*, 14; p. 175..

9. Doxology
Hippolytus, *AT*, p. 32.
Justin, *A*, 65; pp. 17–18.
Addai and Mari, *AM*, p. 37.
AC, pp. 66–67.
Theodore, *T5*, 23; pp. 177–178.

4. Lord's Prayer
Cyril, *M5*, 11; p. 116.

5. Preparation for communion
Serapion, *E*, p. 44.

6. Communion
Cyril, *M5*, 21–22; pp. 116–117.
Ambrose, *S4*, 25; p. 149.
Theodore, *T5*, 24–43; pp. 178–180.

7. Post-Communion
Serapion, *E*, p. 44.

8. Final Blessing and Dismissal
Chrysostum, *A2*, pp. 62–63.

TRANSLATIONS

Ambrose, Saint. *On the Sacraments* in *Theological and Dogmatic Works*. Vol. 44 of *The Fathers of the Church*. Translated by Roy J. Defarrari. Washington: The Catholic University of America Press, 1963.

Cyril of Jerusalem, Saint. *Mystagogical Lectures* in *The Works of Saint Cyril of Jerusalem*. Vol. 2., Vol. 64 of *The Fathers of the Church*. Translated by Leo P. McCauley and Anthony A. Stephenson. Washington: The Catholic University of America Press. 1970.

The Apostolic Tradition, Anaphora of Addai and Mari, Euchologion, Apostolic Constitutions. Deiss, Lucien., ed. *Early Sources of the Liturgy*. Translated by Benet Weatherhead. London: Geoffrey Chapman, 1967.

Didache, in *The Apostolic Fathers*. Vol. 1 of *The Fathers of the Church*. Translated by Francis X. Glimm, Joseph M.-F. Marique, Gerald G. Walsh. New York: CIMA Publishing Company, 1947.

The *Anaphora* of St. Basil and the *Anaphora* of St. John Chrysostom. Hamman, Adalbert., ed. *The Mass: Ancient Liturgies and Patristic Texts*. Translated by Thomas Halton. Staten Island: Alba House, 1967.

John Chrysostom. *Second Instruction* in *Baptismal Instructions*. Vol. 31 of *Ancient Christian Writers*. Translated and edited by Paul W. Harkins. Westminster: The Newman Press, 1963.

Justin, Saint. *First Apology* in *Saint Justin Martyr*. Vol. 6 of *Fathers of the Church*. Translated by Thomas B. Falls. New York: Christian Heritage, Inc., 1948.

Rite of Christian Initiation of Adults. Translation by International Committee on English in the Liturgy, 1974.

Roman Canon. Vagaggini, Cipriano. *The Canon of the Mass and Liturgical Reform*. Translation editor, Peter Coughlan. Staten Island: Alba House, 1967.

Letter to Senarius of John the Deacon. Translated by Edward C. Whitaker, *Documents of the Baptismal Liturgy*. London: S.P.C.K., 1960.

Baptismal Homilies of Theodore Mopsuestia. Translated by Edward Yarnold, *The Awe-Inspiring Rites of Initiation*. Slough: St. Paul Publications, 1971.

BIBLIOGRAPHY

Austin, Gerard. *The Rite of Confirmation: Anointing with the Spirit.* New York: Pueblo Publishing Company, 1985.

Bouley, Allan, ed. *Catholic Rites Today.* Collegeville: Liturgical Press, 1992.

Bouyer, Louis. *Eucharist.* Translated by Charles Underhill Quinn. Notre Dame: University of Notre Dame Press, 1968.

Bradshaw, Paul F. ed. *The Making of Jewish and Christian Worship,* South Bend: University of Notre Dame Press, 1991.

_____Essays on Early Christian Eucharistic Prayers. Collegeville: Liturgical Press, 1997.

Cabie, Robert. *The Eucharist.* Translated by Matthew J. O'Connell. Vol. 2 of *The Church at Prayer: An Introduction to the Liturgy.* Collegeville: The Liturgical Press, 1986.

Chadwick, Henry. *The Early Church.* Middlesex: Penguin Books, Ltd., 1967.

Dix, Gregory. *The Shape of the Liturgy.* Westminster: Dacre Press, l945.

Duffy, Regis A. *On Becoming a Catholic.* New York: Harper and Row, 1984.

Emminghaus, Johannes H. *The Eucharist: Essence, Form, Celebration.* 2nd revised edition by Theodor Maas-Ewerd. Translated by Linda M. Maloney. Collegeville: The Liturgical Press, 1997.

Ganoczy, Alexander. *Becoming Christian: A Theology of Baptism as a Sacrament of Human History.* Translated by John G. Lynch. New York: Paulist Press, 1976.

Guzie, Tad. *The Book of Sacramental Basics.* New York: Paulist Press, 1981.

Jasper, R.C.D., and G. J. Cuming. Translators and editors. *Prayers of the Eucharist.* 3rd ed. New York: Pueblo, 1987.

Johnson, Maxwell, *The Rites of Initiation*: Their Evolution and Interpretation. Collegeville: Liturgical Press, 1999.

Jones, Cheslyn, Geoffrey Wainwright and Edward Yarnold. *The Study of Liturgy*. New York: Oxford University Press, 1978.

Jungmann, Joseph A. *The Mass of the Roman Rite*. Translated by Francis A. Brunner. 2 Vols. New York: Benzinger Brothers, 1951, 1955.

Kavanagh, Aidan. *The Shape of Baptism: The Rite of Christian Initiation*. New York: Pueblo Publishing Company, 1978.

Kilmartin, Edward. Robert J. Daly, ed. *The Eucharist in the West: History and Theology*. Collegeville: Liturgical Press, 1998.

LaVerdiere, Eugene. *The Eucharist in the New Testament and the Early Church*. Collegeville: Liturgical Press, 1996

Marsh, Thomas. *Gift of Community: Baptism and Confirmation*. Wilmington: Michael Glazier, 1984.

Martos, Joseph. *Doors to the Sacred*. New York: Doubleday and Company, Inc., 1982.

Mazza, Enrico. *Mystagogy*. Translated by Matthew J. O'Connell. New York: Pueblo, 1995.

_____*Origins of the Eucharistic Prayer*. Translated by Matthew J. O'Connell. New York: Pueblo, 1995.

_____*The Celebration of the Eucharist: The Origin of the Rite and the Development of Its Interpretation*. Collegeville: Liturgical Press, 1999.

Metzer, Marcel. *History of the Liturgy: The Major Stages*. Collegeville: Liturgical Press, 1997.

Neunheuser, Burkhard. *Baptism and Confirmation*. Translated by John Jay Hughes. New York: Herder and Herder, 1964.

Rordorf, Willy, et al. *The Eucharist of the Early Christians*. Translated by Matthew J. O'Connell. New York: Pueblo Publishing Company, 1978.

Schulz, Hans-Joachim. *The Byzantine Liturgy*. Translated by Matthew J. O'Connell. New York: Pueblo Publishing Company, 1986.

Searle, Mark. *Christening: The Making of Christians*. Collegeville: The Liturgical Press, 1980.

Taft, Robert. *The Byzantine Rite: A Short History*. Collegeville: Liturgical Press, 1992.

Turner, Paul. *Sources of Confirmation from the Fathers Through the Reformers*. Collegeville: Liturgical Press, 1998.

Wegman, Herman. *Christian Worship in East and West: A Study Guide to Liturgical History*. Translated by Gordon W. Lathrop. New York: Pueblo Publishing Company, 1985.

INDEX OF TOPICS

INDEX OF NAMES